W9-AXD-676

BLACK SMART

BLACK-SMART is a collection of short and simple essays concerning Black People's responses to racism in the United States of America. BLACK-SMART points out how small changes on the part of Black People can lead to big changes in Black-white relationships.

Edited by

Mba Mbulu and Bomani Sekou

Published by "The People"
Made in the United States of America

BLACK-SMART

Edited by Mba Mbulu and Bomani Sekou

Copyright © 1995 "The People" All Rights Reserved

These essays were originally written for *"The People's Newsletter"*,
and remain the property of Mba Mbulu,
who retains sole and exclusive rights
over their use and exploitation. All rights are reserved.

ISBN: 1-883885-09-4

LCIP Pending

We Publish Honest Black Writings. We Are

"The People"

P. O. Box 50334
Washington, D. C. 20091
Special Orders Welcome

THE PEOPLE
Washington, D.C.

TABLE OF CONTENTS

EDITOR'S NOTE #1

Throughout this book [BLACK-SMART], and in all publications of "The People", the term Black People and all terms that refer to all of Us are capitalized. This is because Black philosophy is a philosophy of the group as opposed to a philosophy of the individual. To Us, the group, the Race, is supreme; Its identification and survival are of major concern and consideration. Therefore, whatever is referred to It is capitalized. This is in contrast to the philosophy of white people, which stresses the individual ("I") and capitalizes terms which refer to the individual while failing to capitalize terms that refer to the whole group. The difference in this particular aspect of philosophy indicates how basic the differences are between Black People and white people.

EDITOR'S NOTE #2

You might not like what is written here; the uncompromising language of "The People's Newsletter" raised the ire of many of its readers, be they Black or white, male or female, straight, gay or whatever. People in America are poorly educated and have trouble dealing with reality.

INTRODUCTION

BLACK-SMART is a compilation of short essays that were initially printed in "The People's Newsletter" in the mid- to late- 1970s. As such, they were intended for the eyes of Black People only. Now they are being issued for the eyes of all people in this country and abroad, but particularly here because all Americans need to be Black-smart, lest the issue of race result in the carnage of millions of innocent lives.

Not that I expect white people to read these essays or any serious writings by Black persons. Why? Because white people don't read Black books, and that's one of the reasons America has a future full of Hell. But that's another book, one that will be complete and available to the public in a matter of months.

At the time these short essays were written, the hope was that the Black masses (regardless of "class") were serious about independence, self-determination and Black Nationhood. This release, BLACK-SMART, entertains the possibility that the Black masses are more inclined to integrate than segregate [in spite of white resistance to integration]. If such is the case, more mutual understanding than I think is possible will have to exist between Blacks and whites, and that understanding can only be approached if each race clearly and unreservedly spills out its feelings and opinions. Anything else will lead to a false sense of secure race relations and ultimately result in racial explosions that could approximate a second civil war. This is particularly true in light of the depressing economic woes America will be forced to confront in the very, very near future.

This, America's economic woes, is one factor Black integrationists need to consider with great care. The recent collapse of state capitalism in the USSR (Russia) could soon be followed by the collapse of private capitalism in the United States. When this happens, the masses of the people will tend to resort to their more primitive instincts, and scapegoats will be sought. Black People have traditionally filled the role of America's scapegoat, and this time the baseness of American whites could be more brutal than ever. Black integrationists had better be prepared to defend themselves. More intelligent Blacks will not only be prepared to defend themselves, they will be looking for opportunities to take the offensive as well. When disaster strikes, when the economy collapses and takes America's lifetime savings and world prestige down with it, America will be up for grabs and in for some major changes (witness the breakup of the USSR, Bosnia, etc.).

Those who are organized will be in a position to gain from America's collapse. Others will suffer to the extreme.

Therefore, We cannot smother Our intelligence nor fail to face up to what Our intelligence reveals. We have to recognize what needs to be done, overcome whatever inertia exists and act accordingly. That is what BLACK-SMART is all about, that is what being Black-smart is all about and that is why all of Us must be Black-Smart.

1994
Washington, D.C.

BLACK-SMART

BLACK

Section One

SMART

BLACK-SMART:
SHORT ESSAYS TOWARD PROGRESS

VOLUME 1

TABLE OF ESSAYS

1. We Have A Lot Of Work To Do, Part 1

Brothers and Sisters, We have been very scientific in Our studies to determine the cause of all of Our misery, and We have correctly concluded that racism and capitalism/imperialism are at the root of this misery. We have discovered that one man's superiority complex and one man's desire to rob and enslave and stagnate humanity in order to deify property and its ownership/hoarding have resulted in a form of living which is characterized by a pathetic lifelessness. We concluded that We could bring an end to this misery by educating all people to the fact that misery, strife, hunger and suffering are necessary if racism and capitalism are to exist and thrive. We applied Our theory, with the effect that no educated person in America is unaware of it. Yet Our suffering has increased. We are starving in the midst of plenty and dying of non-critical diseases in an age when science and medicine can remove a five month old fetus from a woman's womb and sustain it indefinitely. The obvious question is, "Why?".

The answer, by this time to no one's surprise, is just as obvious. We have an understanding of the system which breeds this misery, but We have failed to understand the people who have perpetuated this racist, anti-human monster. We have failed to understand white people. If We had understood them We would not have wasted time pleading to them, criticizing to them and blaming them for what they developed and are continuing to develop. We did these things because We took it for granted that they did not understand the implications and manifestations of racism and capitalism/imperialism. We took it for granted that they did not truly understand what they were doing. We should have been congratulating them because, as Fanon has stated, white people have done what they set out to do and on the whole they have done it well.

Brothers and Sisters, We have a lot of work to do and criticizing white people is no longer a part of that work. They have attempted to destroy the world (themselves included) because it is an almost natural thing for them to do. Destruction is a part of them. If it wasn't, they couldn't do it as much as they do it and then do it again. They have destroyed human beings since time immemorial. They murdered hundreds of millions of Blacks in Africa and forced other Blacks to come to America, where they were worked to death, castrated to death, raped to death and worried to death. They murdered over one million native North Americans at places like Wounded Knee. They murdered over twenty million natives of South America (the Incas and Aztecs, e.g.). They raped and slaughtered millions of Indian and Chinese inhabitants of Asia. They used Jews for target practice, experimented with the atomic bomb on the Japanese people of Hiroshima and Nagasaki and are at present testing the long term effects of advanced chemical warfare and biological warfare on plant and animal life. Worse still, they are using foreign lands, Viet Nam and Cambodia, as testing stations and the people there as guinea pigs. They do it to Us and they do it to themselves. Hitler is proof of that.

So We shouldn't criticize them any longer. We have no more reason to believe that they will be responsible leaders. WE have to assume the responsibility and burden of leadership. WE have to drop Our happy-go-lucky ways and become responsible to Ourselves and the world. We know how much Black People have been conditioned to shun responsibility, but that is beside the point. It is a question of either non-white leadership preparing the masses for the fundamental changes which are necessary or non-white people allowing whites to continue along their path of destruction. WE have a choice to make. WE can either allow white people to continue along their path of ruthless destruction or WE can excite the masses and prepare the masses to bring about the basic economic and political changes which are necessary to end this destruction. The choice is Ours, Brothers and Sisters. We have realized the key to power. We can't blame whitey anymore. We can't blame anyone anymore but Ourselves. If We remain in the ghetto much longer, it will be because We want to remain there.

PEACE be with you, Brothers and Sisters, if you are willing to do what is necessary to get it.

2. We Have A Lot Of Work To Do, Part II

Black People in America have a lot of work to do. In these next three to four years We have to be especially productive because these are the years when We must lay the cultural, social and educational foundation for a Black nation. Now there are some of Us who don't want to hear about a Black nation. Some of Us still think whitey is going to treat Us right by giving Us more equal rights, better jobs, better educational opportunities, better apartments (because housing is out of the question) and a lot of other goodies which tend to make Us better at being passive. To all of you who think that way, we answer that how whitey is going to treat Us isn't the issue anymore. The issue is the development and elevation of a race of people to its proper position in Nature's order of life. The issue is Black pride, Black self-determination, Black liberation. The issue is Black People being responsible to/for all other Black People. The issue doesn't involve whitey at all. Whitey isn't important anymore, and if you are too brainwashed or too afraid to admit or realize this, then you are part of what will become known as Our Black Problem.

There are others of Us who don't want to hear about a Black nation, not because they think whitey is going to treat Us right but because they just don't have the time to help build a nation. Time isn't a problem with the earlier mentioned anti-Black nationalists. These people are educators, entertainers, doctors, politicians, etc., and they don't see what they have to gain from a Black nation. They are selfish, they are brainwashed, and they think they have "made it". This second group of anti-Black nationalists know they haven't made it, but time wont allow them to change the situation. You see, these persons are busy 24 hours a day, 168 hours a week. They are so busy in fact, that to be productive is out of the question. They are busy doing what Charlie orders them to do for forty hours each week, they dress, undress and sleep for 76 hours each week, and they spend the other 52 hours of each week buying clothes and records, looking at articles they wish they could buy, riding around in circles, partying, looking at tv and staying "busy" in other ways. These people don't give a damn about whitey, yet they keep him on top of

BLACK-SMART   15

the world by being unproductive. These persons love Black People but they don't care enough about the Black Race to sacrifice any of their individual pleasures. And individual pleasures, at this point in space and time, are the major obstacles to Black Nationhood.

We wont deal any further with the selfish group of individuals we referred to earlier. If they love whitey and if they think white is right, then they belong exactly where they are (under whitey's right foot). We are concerned however about those Blacks who don't give a damn about whitey, yet act as if they don't give a damn about the Black race either. You people have an important role to play in the liberation of the Black race. You people have to make time to think. You people have to get your thoughts together; you have to place some worthwhile thoughts in that space which was left when you stopped thinking about whitey. You people have to stop so much bull-jiving and stop putting a high value on petty items like shoes, clothes and cars. You people have to stop using all your energy at a party and contribute that energy to a worthwhile Black cause. We don't need any brainwashed Negroes, but We do need Blacks who have washed themselves of whitey's way of doing things. Therefore, you have to take it upon yourself to educate yourself or get someone to educate you; to what is happening, how it is happening, how it is affecting Us and what We need to do to overcome Our obstacles and build. You are the key, Black man or woman, even as you read this letter, and you have to turn yourself on and drive in a positive direction. If you don't do this the Black race will never move, and We'll have no one to blame but Ourselves.

PEACE be with you, Brothers and Sisters, if you are willing to do what is necessary to get it.

3. Some Black Guidelines

Black People need to begin to respect other Black People. This will help Us move and improve more than anything whitey or anyone else can do for Us. We can do more for Ourselves than anybody else can do for Us by changing Our attitudes and changing the way We treat one another. Here are some Black Guidelines:

(1) Before you do anything to another Black person, Stop and think about it. If there is anything you can do to keep from having trouble with your Brothers and Sisters, then do it.

(2) Stop hurting other Black People. What's the use of being badd if all you can do is hurt other Black People?

(3) Brothers, stop beating up on Sisters, and Sisters, stop doing things which could make a Brother beat up on you.

(4) Stop gossiping about Black People. Badmouthing can lead to a negative act (a fight, e.g.), and negative acts can get other Black persons hurt.

(5) Stop cheating and robbing other Blacks. We're already poor and whitey is cheating Us and robbing Us enough, so it doesn't make sense for Us to do it to Ourselves.

(6) Stop ripping Black People off in any way.

(7) Don't gamble if you get mad easily. It could lead to another Black person getting hurt.

(8) Have fun and joke, but don't try to shame Black People or make another Black person mad. It could get another Black person hurt.

(9) We have to talk among Ourselves in order to keep misunderstandings and negative vibes from breaking out. The better We get to know each other, the less the chance that We'll fight one another because of something that was heard.

(10) Remember who your real enemy is. Remember who is causing you and the rest of your family and friends to suffer. We can't get a good job, We can't buy what We need and want and We live in shacks because whitey and some uncle toms are doing Us in. So whenever you feel like fighting or

BLACK-SMART 17

cussing, don't do it to another Black person. Save it for the people who cause all of your problems, big and small, in the first place.

A change of attitudes toward one another is the first big step for Us, Brothers and Sisters. This change of attitude will allow Us to love one another and respect one another. Remember what these guidelines say and be conscious of them at all times. Everything We do from now on will either speed up Our liberation or slow it down. It depends on how We act, and nothing else.

PEACE be with you, Brothers and Sisters, if you are willing to do what is necessary to get it.

BLACK-SMART

4. Concerning Our So-Called Community Organizations

Our so-called community organizations are failing Us (Black People) pitifully these days. Especially is this true in the national capital of white America, where a critical racist attack is confronting an unknowing and apathetic Black community with threats of educational genocide. This attack, if not combatted uncompromisingly by Black People, will immediately stifle the creativity and learning ability of Black children and eventually result in the spiritual genocide of the Black race. We can't let this happen because Black People's spirit, Our natural harmony with the Universe, is the essence of Our being; but the fact that this might happen is proof of the failure of Our so-called community organizations. These organizations, supposedly in the vanguard (front) of Our move toward progress, have failed to embrace the importance of working for the community in the community. Working in the community requires time, and Our so-called community organizations have failed to give that time; they have failed to take the time necessary to make Black People aware of what's happening around the world, and they have failed to take the time necessary to rid Black People of Our apathy. They have failed to take the time necessary to lay the foundation which would enable Black People in the District of Columbia to realize how critical an issue such as who controls Our mental development is to Us. Because of Our so-called community organizations' failure in this respect, Black People in the District of Columbia are not able to realize when they are being attacked and/or they (We) are not able to realize the full implications of these attacks. As a result, We don't defend Ourselves.

It must be said that Our so-called community organizations have lost their revolutionary initiative. They have lost their will to struggle with the people (who are slow to respond) and choose instead to struggle for the people. In their desire to struggle for the people, they leave the people. They begin to appeal instead to those forces which oppress the people and, not surprisingly, become incapable of challenging those oppressive forces. They continue to pay lip service to revolutionary ideas but in fact (practice) they are counter-

BLACK-SMART 19

revolutionary/counter-progressive because they are no longer in touch with the concept of a people's movement and they are out of sympathy with the process through which a people prepare themselves for liberation and self-determination.

These so-called community organizations fail to adhere to the doctrine that the people are the source of power. This partly explains why they act as they do. But even more important in explaining why they leave the people is the development of chauvinistic or selfish concerns within the organizations themselves. Some organization members begin to want to see the results of their work. As a result, instead of reviewing time as their companion they subconsciously begin to think of time as their enemy. They begin to feel that they have to get to where they are going in a hurry, and that the people are holding them back. They begin to desire to see the fruit of their labor, and this desire leads these so-called community organizations to accommodate and compromise with Our oppressors. At times this results in immediate visible gains, but in essence it achieves two counter-revolutionary/counter-progressive results: (1) It leaves the so-called community organization impotent because the organization has abandoned the source of its power (the people). This in turn allows the oppressor to maintain himself at the expense of an oppressed people for a much longer period of time and, (2) It eliminates an alternative model to which a number of people can turn in case they rid themselves of the oppressor's mental yoke. These so-called community organizations (which accommodate the people's oppressors) appear to benefit the people but the fact that less than 50 persons show up to demonstrate against judicial injustice in America in this same area and the fact that less than 700 persons mass on a given day in support of African Liberation is proof that the organizations that are supposedly working for the people are not working with the people. Somewhere down the line these organizations lost their will to bring Our oppressor to his knees. This is a critical loss.

The purpose of a progressive community organization is to heighten the level of consciousness of the people and establish vehicles through which the people can advance quickly once their level of consciousness has reached a

BLACK-SMART

certain height. A progressive community organization should not attempt to prepare people to live in this hell nor make their existence in hell easier to bear. This salves the rebellion potential of the oppressed and therefore helps maintain the reign of the oppressor.

We walk through the Black community. In various places we see organization headquarters but in very few of these places do we see or feel the presence of the organization itself. In even fewer places do we see organization members dealing with the community's inhabitants. When we do see intermingling, we have to wonder if it is done as a matter of course or accidentally.

We have to be positively aggressive with Our people, Brothers and Sisters (whether you be organization members or not). We have to force them to listen and force them to understand. When they fail to respond it is up to us to approach them until they do respond. Their response is necessary, and we must work with them until this response comes as a matter of course. Then, and only then, will changes come about which will benefit the masses of the people because they will be accompanied by a mass frame of mind which, whether accompanied by a physical force or not, will shake the very foundation of the oppressor and his power. You see, the oppressor's power depends upon and is in fact the ignorance and lack of awareness of the masses (those he oppresses). Remove the lack of awareness of the masses and you at the same time remove the power of the oppressor. It's as simple as that.

But all simple things can not be brought about right away. It sometimes takes time, a lot of it. Those of Us who are sincere are willing to work as hard as we can with the people and wait for them to respond. If we are unwilling to do this, then we will never lay the type of foundation which is necessary to bring about real changes. Superficial changes, sure, but real changes can never come about unless the people possess a frame of mind that will bring them about.

We say to all of you so-called community organizations: A revolutionary and progressive group should never attempt to work for the people if that work necessitates abandoning the people. The revolutionary organization should not

BLACK-SMART   21

look for quick results but real results. These results might come about during your existence, but they might not. We should not be concerned about that. We should be concerned with educating the people by whatever means necessary. We must work with the people in the streets, in the classrooms, when we confront Our oppressors. If we are sincere about doing this then the people will eventually work for themselves (all of Us). If we are not sincere, then we should stop making use of revolutionary rhetoric which is accompanied by reactionary practices. This tends to confuse and disenchant the people even more and makes the task of the sincere revolutionary that much more difficult.

The People are the power, Brothers and Sisters. Once we make them realize this, the People will end their own oppression.

PEACE be with you, Brothers and Sisters, if you are willing to do what is necessary to get it.

5. Think For Yourself

What is read, what is seen or viewed and what is heard are three factors which weigh heavily as an exploited group attempts to free itself of the exploiters' influences. We should never forget this. What We read in the newspapers and magazines, what We see on the television screen and at the movies and what We hear on the radio are calculated attempts by those who own these vehicles to keep Us from realizing what is important and what is not important, to manipulate the way We think about them (Our exploiters), and to manipulate the way We think about persons and/or organizations that oppose what they are trying to do. Everything We read, everything We see and everything We hear should be carefully analyzed by each of Us before We conclude that one thing is good or beneficial and another thing is causing trouble or is "just a lot of jive". Every attempt to influence Us, be it Black-, Red- or white-originated, should be carefully analyzed by each of Us. Why? Because We cannot trust them, and because IT IS IMPORTANT THAT EACH OF US GET INTO THE HABIT OF DOING HIS OR HER OWN THINKING.

Some of Us find it difficult to accept the fact that it is not the purpose of those who take advantage of Us to tell Us the truth. As a result, We accept what We read in the various newspapers, We accept what Walter Cronkite and Eric Sevareid show Us and We accept what the radio stations tell Us. We have no logical reason for doing so. And, on another level, We describe Jaws and Love Story as "good" books, We feel that Kojak is a "good" cop, "Good Times" is a "good" television show and We listen to the "good" music WOL plays (and keep up with what's happening at the same time). We seem to forget that good books should be real as well as entertaining, good cops put Us in jail when We are forced to rob and steal to survive, no family which lives in the ghetto constantly has a good time and, as far as WOL is concerned, if it's not a party or a concert it is definitely not what's happening. We lose when We forget these things, Brothers and Sisters. Once again We lose.

We accept their news stories although We know how much they lie. We watch what is done in that fairyland called tv and then try to do the same thing on the real streets of Blackbottom, in our split level homes or at Our de-segregated jobs. They have put Us to sleep, and it is time for Us to wake up. It is time for Us to start acting according to what We know and to start learning about the things We don't know.

We don't live in a studio, Brothers and Sisters, and neither Walter Cronkite nor the owner of the Washington Post or Star is Our friend. We know the water is poisoned so it doesn't make sense to drink it even when We're thirsty because it is going to kill Us in the long run. But it's your choice Brother, and yours too Sister. What are you going to do?

PEACE be with you, Brothers and Sisters, if you are willing to do what is necessary to get it.

6. The Press: Dr. Jekyll Is Hyding

In the 1770s a social, economic and political relationship had developed between Great Britain and her American colonies which established Great Britain as a dominant tyrannical force. As a result, many of the colonial people began developing feelings of resentment toward the mother country (Great Britain). As time passed they tired of the constant tyranny of King George to the point where the most politically aware among them felt that something should be done to stop that tyranny for once and for all. These men were in favor of opposing tyranny with arms if necessary, but in order to do this effectively they had to overcome a major obstacle. They knew that most of the colonial people would sympathize with their cause because it was a just cause, but they also realized that this sympathy would not develop into actual open support unless some vehicle was used to popularize their just cause on a mass level. They needed a vehicle which would transport similar ideas to persons in all parts of the colony at the most opportune times. This vehicle would be used to champion the cause of resisting tyranny and make the people fond of those who resist tyranny and deathly critical of all others. In short, they needed a vehicle which would render the masses of the people mentally free of Great Britain. This vehicle was the press (news media).

The Revolutionary War period adorned the press with an esteem and trust from the people which few other institutions in America could match. It was the standard bearer of those who struggled against oppression. It was a call for liberty from those who were the victims of tyranny. It would be the guardian of democracy and freedom which all people crave for because it would always be a tool for the people used by the people to the benefit of the people. When all other attempts at redress failed, one would rest assured that he could report his story to the press and have it read throughout the country by interested persons who would adopt his cause and make Justice stand.

Two hundred years later a social, economic and political system has been established in America which corrupts the entire known world. It is a system

BLACK-SMART 25

which represents a few individuals who are not concerned with the benefit of mankind but with the benefit of certain kinds of men. It is a system which places little, if any, value on terms like democracy, freedom and justice, but champions instead the quest for profits, power and the satisfaction of all types of negative aggressions. It is a system which is inherently tyrannical and it operates beyond the scope and understanding of most people because it does not want its true colors revealed to the masses of the people. It intends instead to deceive the people by brainwashing them into thinking that self-preservation is the first law of Nature and that unemployment is necessary in any advanced economic structure. It intends to rid the people of their love for real values like Freedom, Respect and Justice by inserting a desire for material objects such as homes and cars in their places. It intends to render people politically obtuse (ignorant) by focussing their attention on such intellectual teasers as astrology, junk literature and sensational motion pictures, and denying them access to any quality which might bring about or stimulate any positive mental activity. It intends to rid the people of their creative genius while simultaneously conditioning the people to the virtues of "Do as you are instructed to do". In short, this system intends to scientifically completely enslave more than 99% of the known world's human population in order to insure that the less than one percent of the population which it represents can enjoy the fruit of their thievery, murder and deceit without having to worry about a destructive reaction from the people they mercilessly victimize. And what are they already using to accomplish this end? The PRESS (media)!!!

Since the 1770s the same press which was hailed as the guardian of a democratic people has been usurped and expanded by that group of individuals which is threatened by democracy. That group has since that time changed the press from a savior of the people to a threat to the people. That group which intends to enslave humanity has used money and force to eliminate the free press and has replaced it with a controlled written, oral and visual communications network which does not have as its purpose the telling of the truth. Its purpose is not to report the news but to dictate the selfish views of the new King Georges. By gradually changing the press from Dr. Jekyll to

BLACK-SMART

Mr. Hyde, the new owners hope that most people will not notice its new purpose and therefore not lose their esteem for it and their trust in it (translated: people will continue to believe what the press tells them). But, as before, there are today politically alert persons who see through this diabolical scheme, who see the changes the press has been taken through and who also see the eventual posture the press will be forced to assume. Less and less news, more and more self-serving views. Less and less news about what positively affects the people, more and more views about crime in the streets. Less and less news about the Malcolm Xs and the Barbara Sizemores, more and more views about social security, food stamps and the criminal mentality. Less and less news that will help Us grow, more and more views that will freeze Our development by cutting off Our tendencies to communicate with others honestly. Less and less news about police brutality and the disgrace of poverty, more and more views about law enforcement and "free enterprise". Less and less news about adequate housing and proper health care, more and more views about the rights of landlords and insurance indemnities. Less and less news, more and more views. Less and less news, more and more views. WAKE UP, PEOPLE, WAKE UP`!!!!!

PEACE be with you, Brothers and Sisters, if you are willing to do what is necessary to get it.

7. Your Choice To Make

Are you content with adjusting to the warp of a murderer, kidnapper and liar, Brothers and Sisters? Do you want to continue this rat race for "the *necessary* things"? Does the "general acceptance and widespread practice of the more deranged products of western culture" suit your aims in life as a Black person? or are you sane enough to consider being what these Europeans in America call a "subversive" or "irresponsible person"? Think about it People. You can either adapt America's barbarism and spread this madness We live in or you can adopt the principles which, once activated, will bring about a sane and healthy society which will benefit mankind. Is it the one, or is it the other? Brothers and Sisters, it is your choice to make.

PEACE be with you, Brothers and Sisters, if you are willing to do what is necessary to get it.

8. How Far, Recognition?

It is natural for Us to want other people to recognize Us, Brothers and Sisters. It is natural for Us to want to prove to all people that We are as "good" as they are. It is natural that We should want them to admit that We know how to act properly, that We know how to add and subtract, that We know how to make an intelligent decision, etc. It is natural that We should want them to know that We are not dirty people and that We don't rob and steal and cheat as a matter of course. We want them to know that We can live in the suburbs without contaminating its attractiveness, that We can work at a desk just as efficiently as anyone else and that We can direct an organization or business and represent numbers of people just as well as anyone else. We _have_ to prove to other people, especially those who think they are superior to Us, that We are as "good" as they are. For this reason We have continually sought the recognition of the white race.

Members of the white race have charged that they were/are superior to Us. To support their contention they boasted that We could not read, write or talk properly, and that We did not understand simple arithmetic. We learned to read well enough to understand America's judicial system and become lawyers and judges; to write well enough to become poets and authors, and to issue magazines and newspapers; and to talk properly enough to report the news on television and speak to thousands of students on America's most respected college campuses. To prove that We could add and subtract We became cashiers at department stores and clerks at the largest agencies of the U.S. government. We went even further! We used Our mathematical genius combined with Our knowledge of electricity and developed the automatic traffic light; and We studied the heavenly bodies, calculated their courses and predicted eclipses. We planned the city of the District of Columbia, became "sought after" engineers, and discovered how to refine sugar. Still, We failed to get the recognition of those who enslaved Us.

We have proven beyond any doubt that We are capable of doing anything anyone else does, Brothers and Sisters. Therein lies the rub! We have proven to the white race that We can talk like them, calculate like them, do their work efficiently and live according to their standards. In short, We have proven that We can overcome all obstacles and adapt Our tendencies to their way of life. What We have failed to prove, however, is that We are capable of breaking with the sickness that is basic to their way of life. We have failed to prove that We can reject them and establish a social, economic and governmental order based on Our tendencies which other people would want to imitate. Until We do this We will never receive the respect which human beings should receive.

We have to de-brainwash Ourselves, Brothers and Sisters. We can do this by first asking Ourselves if We are in fact inferior. We must ask Ourselves if the white race possesses characteristics or tendencies which any civilized people would want to imitate, and if they don't We must ask Ourselves why We continue to imitate them. We have to determine if We should want them to recognize Us! Should We want barbarians to recognize Us? After all, man is human only to the extent to which he tries to impose his existence on another man in order to be recognized by him. We know well that domination is what the white man seeks primarily, not recognition.

Another question We must ask Ourselves, collectively and individually, is "Are We human?" Humans attempt to impose their existence on another human in order to be recognized by him/her. All We have attempted to do is surrender Our existence in order to better imitate another man's existence. It follows then that We don't deserve to be recognized because We haven't attempted to impose Our existence, Our way of life or Our "reason for being" upon other peoples of the world.

What are We all about, Brothers and Sisters? A boring eight hours a day job and 24 hours a day of frustration caused by petty-mindedness, selfishness, lack of concern for others, lack of justice, hunger, poverty and unnecessary disease? Or can We express life (Our existence) with a lot less tension and uncertainty/insecurity? Do We care about Ourselves and the young and unborn Black babies who wont give a damn about whitey but will end up in whitey's prisons or doing what whitey wants them to do because We failed to prepare

30   BLACK-SMART

them to do otherwise?

We have to build and make operable some vehicles which will carry Our young to positive points Brothers and Sisters. Whitey's vehicles will not benefit Our young, so We must stop bringing his vehicles into Our life and stop imitating them in any manner. We as a group need to go through a lot of social changes, but each of Us needs to go through some individual/personal changes as well in order to make it easier for the social changes We must instill (among Ourselves) to hold ground and grow.

Our vehicles, Brothers and Sisters, Our institutions and Our way of life! Nothing less will do!!!

PEACE be with you, Brothers and Sisters, if you are willing to do what is necessary to get it.

9. Take A Look At Yourself

Black People, We have been thrown by strange historical sequences into the hands of capitalists/racists. We have been the objects of poverty and charity and unemployment and public assistance, etc., all because We are despised. We have been the toys of rich people and the scapegoats of all others. It is now time that We no longer play those roles. We must awaken. We must assert Ourselves and be objects no longer. We must scale the ladder of humanness and cover it with Our humanity.

We must cleanse Ourselves of the evils of "get and grab". We must erase the impulses which drive Us to privately hoard tangibles and intangibles which make life livable. We must rid Ourselves of their "rake and scrape" and "squeeze and cheat" mentality, and search instead for Our salvation, a salvation which will be found in human brotherhood, equality of opportunity and work—not for individual wealth and security but for the wealth and security of Us all. We must carefully choose Our "brothers" by recognizing that Our natural friends (though not yet allies) are not the rich and the middle class but the poor, not the great and their helpers but the masses, not the employers, the overseers/supervisors nor the union representatives but the employees, and We must realize that Our goal lies not in personal wealth, power, oppression and/or snobbishness, but in helpfulness, efficiency, service and self respect.

We must realize that We will not get Our salvation by wishing for it or simply because We want it, Brothers and Sisters. We must realize that We will not get Our salvation by joining with forces which seem to be more powerful than We seem to be. We must accept the fact that WE must do what is necessary to get Our salvation, and that We must do it Ourselves. If We feel the need to exclude capitalism from Our organizational processes, We must do so; not because We are against individual initiative but because capitalism itself is anti-social (against the masses). If We feel the need to exclude whites from Our organizational processes, We must do so; not because We are racists but because We accept the fact that whites and their institutions are racist and elitist, and that nothing is going to change their racist and elitist character for centuries to come. If We feel the need to attack Islam and/or Christianity, We must do so; not because We are anti-religion or prefer one religion over another, but because neither of these religions is native to Us and both have been used to enslave Us. If We feel the need to criticize groups which attempt to help Black People, We must do so; not because We always doubt their sincerity but because We question their goals and/or their tactics.

In order to progress We have to take some cold, analytical looks at Ourselves, Black People. We have to realize that We (you included) have been half-stepping, whether We intended to half-step or not. We have to realize that We have been rationalizing (attempting to justify) Our failures and shortcomings, whether We intended to rationalize or not. We must realize that up to this point most of Our "new" or "radical/militant" ideas and most of what We have attempted to do has been dictated by what whitey does, what whitey attempts to do or what whitey attempts to undo. In order to progress We have to stop responding, We have to stop reacting. We have to start issuing the first stimulus—We have to act!

We have to devise a strategy People, a plan; and organize Our activities around that plan. Without it all We do will be incidental and short lived. To illustrate this We should view the influx of white people back into the inner cities. Already this process is in full swing in the District of Columbia, which was almost 80% Black at the turn of the decade (1970). Blacks, though concerned about this white invasion, are helpless to prevent it because Black People have no plan, neither short nor long term, which includes the District (or any other area for that matter) and would insure continued Black domination. Consequently, Blacks are unable to initiate programs or policies based on Black goals, but react instead to proposals which whites make because they know whites see control of the inner cities as vital to the furtherance of white superiority/domination.

(Incidentally, Blacks in the cities should not expect their councilmen to come up with a Black plan. Their admiration of whitey leaves them incapable of doing anything other than imitating whitey or seeking whitey's approval.)

We need to _act_, Brothers and Sisters. We need to establish a base from which We can attack some goals if not Our enemies. We must do this consciously and scientifically in order to "insure our physical survival, our spiritual freedom and our social growth." If not, We (the babies included) die, Brothers and Sisters, WE DIE!

PEACE be with you, Brothers and Sisters, if you are willing to do what is necessary to get it.

10. The Vote

"Yes, these old folks had a dream book, but the pages went blank and it failed to give them the number." R. Ellison

It's an election year, 1976. It is also the year of the "bicentennial". They (whites) are celebrating 200 years of freedom, and 200 years of violence and "benign neglect" toward Black men, Red men—toward all non-white peoples. They are the ones who stole this land twice and they are the ones who refuse to give up the "freedom" which those thefts allow them. The "bicentennial" is their bicentennial, and they are the only ones who should be celebrating its arrival.

But it's an election year, 1976. It is a time when people in America cast ballots on questions which are strictly American. It is a time when a people participates in a political process which recognizes that all of them are of the same family, and are of the same nation with common problems. It is a time when a people chooses one of several candidates because that one is representative of a frame of mind which will attempt to eliminate the common problems which afflict the "common people".

The "common people" in America are all white and their common problem is getting a labor force which will support their economy and allow them to live a life of ease and comfort. Until this problem is solved, they will elect new schemers (representatives) every two, four or six years because that is what the vehicle they structured (the constitution) calls for.

Black People in America are not of the "common people". The common people conduct themselves according to a general outline called the constitution, but other people don't. Special rules have to be developed for other people which guarantee them special rights like "civil rights" and "voting rights". These rights are special because they are temporary and conditional. They might be taken away at any time because they apply to non-permanent residents who are not generally accepted as part of the "common people".

However, Black People do play a role in America's "common problem".

As a matter of fact, from the point of view of the "common people" Black People are the "common problem". The common people can't live in ease and comfort because Black People refuse to provide the land and labor which could elevate whites to Easy Street. What's more, the Blacks insist on clamoring about things such as justice, equality, socialism and humanity. This produces slight disorders (other problems) among the common people (like widespread poverty among whites, police brutality against whites, astronomical food and insurance costs, etc.) because they have to sacrifice some of their own goodies and give them to the Blacks (anything to stop that protest noise). These disorders are not basic, however. They will disappear as soon as the "common problem" is solved.

The experts among the common people have determined that the common problem can be solved in either of two ways. It can be solved by physically eliminating those special people who refuse to work for the good of the common people or it can be solved by forcing all special people to surrender their land and labor into the hands of the common people. But who among the common people can make either choice a reality? The common people can't agree, so they go to the polls to determine who the majority of them feels can get the job done.

Special people can voice their opinion (vote) on the issue also. The common people agreed to allow this with the provision that special people stick strictly to the issue (don't make any suggestions). Those who are unwilling to stick to the issue need not vote because the vote does not recognize anything but the issue.

What does this mean to Black People in America? We have the choice of voting or not voting, but which should it be? If We vote We might possibly elect some individual who sympathizes with Our desire to live, someone who might attempt to improve Our lot and protect Us or "empower" Us. But when We vote We simultaneously admit that We should either leave the world or submit Our labor and land (Africa, Caribbean, etc.) to those who want to reap without sowing. We admit that the question the common people seek to resolve is a valid question; that some people have to be enslaved and exploited so that others might live comfortably. And, We alienate Our Blackness when We vote by denying the need for its existence. We help to establish a single American people based upon only what is American (white), and We disregard everything else.

Black People in America who vote for Ford or Carter or whoever show a profound lack of understanding of the problems which confront Black People in America and a criminal ignorance of Our self-determining aspirations as well. Participating in the vote means tacitly recognizing that We, Black People, belong to and share the fruit of America's efforts. It is tacitly recognizing that We don't need to exist because the common people will care for Us, discuss the budget and make investments for Us and urge that Africa and other Black lands not be interfered with.

We shouldn't want the "common people" to do anything for Us. We can do for Ourselves. We need first to demonstrate Our will to be Us by not tacitly demonstrating that We want to be a part of them. Then We can become Us by participating in political actions which are intended to erect and institutionalize Our values and priorities; political actions which refuse to even admit that America's common people are worthy of Our recognition or are strong enough to hold Us back.

PEACE be with you, Brothers and Sisters, if you are willing to do what is necessary to get it.

11. Opposites That Don't Attract

White people are opposed to the very idea of Us, Brothers and Sisters; not so much because Black People have weight and occupy space but because Black People represent a spiritual and mental force which opposes their insanity. We should never fail to have this in mind; that Black People are a threat to whites because they, whites, have made it so, if for no other reason. They cannot see Us being Ourselves without simultaneously feeling Us rejecting them and desiring to get them back for what they have done to Us. Remember that! If they "like" you, then it is because you do what they want to see you do; if they don't "like" you, it is because they feel threatened because you don't try to make them feel comfortable.

To be Black or not to be Black; that is the question that confronts each and all of Us today. If We want to integrate, if we feel We have something to prove to them, if We talk softly when one of them approaches or if We feel We need them in order to advance, then We have chosen not to be Black. On the other hand, if We take the attitude that they have something to prove to Us, that they need to integrate with Us for their survival, that they need Us in order to progress and that We have no reason to fear what they hear Us say, e.g., then We have chosen to be Ourselves/Black. The choice is simple.

What We choose will express how We feel about their claims of superiority. If We play their game because it is their game, We at the same time admit that they are superior to Us. But if We attempt to do things Our way according to a set of values and principles which are Ours, then We at the same time challenge their claims of superiority.

How We act when dealing with whitey, no matter how trivial the dealing might seem, will determine how whitey will act when he deals with Us. If We smile when there is nothing to smile about (or because you feel whitey wants you to smile), or fail to demand that which is rightfully Ours, then We have demonstrated a lack of racial- and self-esteem. Whites realize this and treat Us (you) accordingly. However, when We (you) determine how We respond to whatever, regardless of who is around, and when We demand that

BLACK-SMART

which is rightfully Ours, then whitey treats Us with respect because he knows We (you) will not tolerate any disrespect.

Do We demand respect by asserting Our right to be Black? or do We prepare a grim future for Black babies by singing, dancing, praying, damning whitey and not laying the foundation for Black institutions?

We have a view from the bridge Brothers and Sisters, and We know what pitfalls to avoid. Let Us be about the business of avoiding them.

PEACE be with you, Brothers and Sisters, if you are willing to do what is necessary to get it.

12. Mind Power, Part 1

Time is the factor which separates the revolutionaries from the reactionaries. Time reveals who is serious about nationhood and who is not. Time reveals those of Us who are "for real" about Our Blackness and segregates those who rant and rave and use Blackness as a platform aimed at relieving their individual frustrations and anxieties. Time, Brothers and Sisters, time. Time will tell.

Vision is necessary if We are to stand the test of time. Vision enables Us to peek into the future, to see where We are going and to prepare for the obstacles which are going to temporarily hold Us back. If We can't see these things (obstacles and victories) beforehand, We will become disenchanted and use any setback as proof of the hopelessness of Our efforts, thereby excusing Ourselves from any further involvement.

You can't see into the future with your eyes, Brothers and Sisters. You have to use your mind. But your mind must first be developed. Anyone can see from one day to the next, but this short vision will not prepare you to deal with a struggle which spans generations. To do this you have to understand, to the core, what has happened and what is happening.

We are looking for people who are prepared to take the time necessary to bring about fundamental changes in the way Black People think and act; in Our value system. When we say time we don't necessarily mean contributing two or three hours a day to "the cause" or attending some meetings, but working with the knowledge that you have to continue working although it might be years or decades before you see any results. This means preparing yourself and getting others to help prepare you. It means getting a clear understanding of what is going on, getting a thorough understanding of what it takes to change what is going on, planning toward this change and initiating this plan/change. We are going to have to bring these changes about, Brothers and Sisters. We must realize this. WE are going to have to prepare, WE are going to have to act. Either without the other will be counter-productive and destructive.

40 **BLACK-SMART**

An idealist is able to see the future because he/she understands the past and the present. Join the idealists, Brothers and Sisters. Open your mind and let developing Blackness enter it, and struggle with US for a human tomorrow.

PEACE be with you, Brothers and Sisters, if you are willing to do what is necessary to get it.

13. Mind Power, Part II

Revolution, like slavery, is an attitude of mind. A person remains a slave because he/she decides to not seek an alternative (choice). A person becomes a revolutionary because he/she assumes a frame of mind which calls for revolutionary, progressive practices.

Principles create revolutionaries, Brothers and Sisters. A process takes place which results in certain values becoming as much a part of a person as are his eyes or ears. That process, which many times begins as an individual reaction, develops into a universal consciousness and concern for the plight of mankind. It forces the individual to do what is practical and necessary to bring about a way of living which guarantees to each individual that which is due him/her as a member of the human family.

The Black race must become a race of revolutionaries. We must rid Ourselves of the poison that enslavement has left in Our heads. We must break the trend toward acquisitiveness which has become dominant among Us, and We must break the desire to dominate others which seems to be more and more responsible for Our (each of Us) actions. We have to stop being individuals—anti-social beings—and start being humans.

Until institutions are established which encourage mass revolutionary development it is up to each of Us to discipline himself and steer himself toward a revolutionary frame of mind. All of Us can't wait for someone else to guide Us along. When one of Us has spare time, instead of taking a drink, listening to the radio or looking for some fun, that person should make himself aware of Our history (all 7000 recorded years), the histories of other peoples, and fundamental laws which should be applied universally. The universal laws are particularly important because they prepare Us to deal with right and wrong as absolute values, as rules which do not change because of what a person has to gain or lose materially.

If you feel you have to hoard wealth in order to live after your working days are over or if you are afraid to stop working for any valid reason, then you recognize that the system which presently controls your life is anti-social and therefore anti-you. Don't remain a willing part of such a system. Free your mind of it. If you feel there is no hope for you, at least do what is necessary to insure that your/Our young don't get caught in the same hopeless position. Start laying a foundation that will insure that they possess a frame of mind which will not only benefit Black People, but all progressive peoples.

We have to work, but it is imperative that those of Us who work be spiritually and mentally prepared to do so. Needless to say, all of Us will have to work soon.

PEACE be with you, Brothers and Sisters, if you are willing to do what is necessary to get it.

14. Basics, Part 1

We have to start dealing with basics, Brothers and Sisters. We must do so if We are ever going to think properly (analytically), act intelligently (to bring about positive, non-random results) and create (values, institutions, a nation, etc.). We must do so if We expect to become self-determining. We must do so if We expect to reach Our potential and make progressive contributions to the family of humanity.

Basics are roots. They are principles (fundamental, essential laws). They explain what is at the core of an idea, an issue, an institution. They explain what a creation (an idea or institution) is all about; how it got started, how it developed, what it meant to do or represent, how it meant to do it. Only after considering points such as these can We understand a creation's purpose. Only after answering questions such as these can We understand what is going on.

To understand basics We must be able to think properly, to be analytical. Thoughts are ideas, and since We are at a thinking stage in Our development We must concern Ourselves with ideas. Since all actions stem from ideas, it is necessary that We understand what We think and why We think what We think.

Ideas are mental conceptions. Ideas are notions. Ideas are also impressions. This is important to Us because impressions many times have no substantial basis, but they oftentimes determine what We do. This is unfortunate because what We do, individually and collectively, should be based on an understanding of what has confronted Us—of what We are dealing with. Without such an understanding, what We do or refuse to do is just as likely to harm Us as it is to benefit Us.

Our experience in America has forced Us and nudged Us into the habit of attempting to deal with those things which confront Us without getting a basic understanding of what those things are all about. For instance, We have been told (directly and indirectly) that knowing how to tell time, how to drive a car, how to spend money and how to vote, among other things, will make Our life easier. As a result, We become satisfied when We learn to do these

BLACK-SMART

things. We fail to realize that We should seek knowledge of how to build a clock, how a car operates, how to develop an economy and how to form a government as well. Moreover, Our experiences in America have forced and nudged Us into the habit of not seeking an understanding of those things which affect Our life. Therefore We are unable to break those things down, reproduce them, destroy them and/or create something which can replace them. This is unfortunate. That lack of understanding leaves Us unable to create, and the inability to create or produce leaves Us in a position of depending upon others. If such a dependency is vital to Our survival, then whether We survive or not can depend upon the whims or tendencies of a group (or individual) which is not intimately concerned with Our welfare.

Please don't misinterpret what has been said, Brothers and Sisters. We aren't encouraging all Black persons to study clock-making or mechanics because these skills will not determine whether each of Us survives or not. But economics (not money) is a question of survival, as is politics (not voting). Therefore it is necessary that all of Us study and attempt to understand these functions. It is necessary that all of Us study and attempt to understand all functions (things) which are vital to Our survival.

So We have to create a thirst for knowledge. We have to seek various ideas and explanations and explore them. We have to develop Our mental powers because people who are mentally developed realize the importance of exploring all types of possibilities. Why do they do this exploring? Because they know that the conclusions they come to will determine how they act, and they want to act in a manner which will most likely bring about a result they desire; a result which is going to benefit them and the people they care about.

Ideas are therefore very important. The process of thinking and attempting to understand is very important. Getting to the core of anything which is going to affect you/Us is very important. Remember that.

We have already pointed out that all actions stem from ideas. If We think intelligently, if We understand what is being done, We will act intelligently also. If We don't understand what is being done We wont be able to act intelligently because We will not have the slightest idea of what Our action is going to result in.

What is an intelligent act? An intelligent act is one which is intended to bring about positive, non-random results. Positive because they are progressive; non-random because they are not isolated and do not benefit just a handful of individuals. They are intended to benefit a people, your people, because your people are capable of setting a marvelous example which other peoples of the world can pattern their life-styles after. They will pattern their life-style after the symbols which are associated with your people, but most important is that other people will pattern themselves after institutions which your people and your contributions have created. These institutions will include values (how We act toward one another; how We treat one another; how We treat other people), buildings (centers for mental development, centers for medical care and advancement, etc.), an economic structure, a political structure and many other tangible and intangible institutions which could form a spiritual nation, and later a nation as most people see nations. But before any of that can happen, before any type of real progress (progress which stands the test of time) can be made, We have to deal with and get an understanding of basic ideas, concepts, whatever.

Start dealing with basics right now, Brothers and Sisters. See if you have an understanding of what you are about. See how well, how independently, you are thinking. Do you control your thought patterns, therefore your destiny, even a little bit? Be honest with yourself. Seek to change yourself and help all of Us survive and thrive in the process. Get down to the core Brother, and you too Sister; of Us and of things which affect you and Us. If you don't you will have left yourself and Us open to the threat of enslavement and oppression.

PEACE be with you, Brothers and Sisters, if you are willing to do what is necessary to get it.

BLACK-SMART

15. Basics, Part II

In Part 1 it was stressed that We have to start dealing with basics, individually and collectively. When We talk, We have to talk basics. When We listen, We have to listen for basics. When We act, a basic understanding must inspire that act. We have to break each thing down to the core, find out what it is all about and act accordingly. That is what dealing with basics demands of Us.

You might ask why this is so important. Generally speaking it is important because understanding is the key to acting intelligently, and We can't understand unless We deal on a basic level. More specifically, dealing with basics keeps Us from talking one way and unconsciously acting another way, and it prepares Us to recognize negative forces in Our community which take on a positive appearance. The first enables Us to avoid looking like hypocrites; the second enables Us to deal with fakes (and other things which are negative) in a positive, well-planned manner. For the time being, since many of Us, individually and organizationally, are in an early stage of development, let Us deal with point one.

One of the historical and present tragedies of Black individuals and organizations has been their tendency to consciously and/or unconsciously act in a manner which is contrary to what they seem to teach. We are concerned here with the ones who do so unconsciously, because these are the dedicated Brothers and Sisters who make sincere, though many times misguided, efforts toward improving the plight and condition of all of Us. As such, this message is written with them in mind.

When attempting to work for the benefit of the Black community, or any community, it is important that you understand why you feel the need to put forth your energies. This involves understanding the force(s) which has left your community in need of help. It is also important that you understand what you want to do and how you want to do it. Additionally, and just as important, is that you have an understanding of what you don't want to do and how you don't want to act. These are critical, Black People, because they provide

Us with a basis for preciseness of action which does not contradict or de-emphasize the principles which originally motivated Us. More simply put, understanding these basic factors will keep Us/you from unintentionally preaching what We don't practice and/or practicing what We don't preach.

For example, if a group gets together and forms a community organization, the primary concern of that group should be the community. In all considerations the community should come first. If the organization decides it can best help the community by relieving the economic pressures which this system places on it, then it initiates, for example, what have become known as survival programs. Through these as many persons as possible are provided with necessities which make the hell they go through a little bit easier to bear.

But how does that organization acquire the necessities (goods and services/know-how) it needs to help the community? And, how does it go about delivering what it has accumulated to the community? If these two questions aren't clearly analyzed and answered by each organization beforehand, that organization might, in its eagerness to help the community, unconsciously use those same forces which were intentionally used earlier to oppress/impoverish the community. Though these forces might be used in ignorance, and though kind and sincere intentions created them, their essence will be the same—community exploitation. Which means their results—community poverty, etc.,—will be the same.

So We have to be certain that We don't use enemies of the community when We attempt to help the community. If an organization has decided that capitalism is bad for the community, it should get a core understanding of capitalism which will enable its members to recognize capitalism however it appears. If an organization has decided that class-consciousness is bad, organization members must be able to recognize that in all its forms. If an organization has decided that exploitation in general is the community's problem, that organization must be able to recognize exploitation in all its forms and degrees. Being able to recognize these negative forces will help Us avoid the use of them when We attempt to do some good. Failure to avoid them could prove catastrophic in the long run.

To deal with basics is a demanding proposition, Brothers and Sisters. Since We have a demanding problem, demanding measures and solutions are necessary. Anything less, as far as Our work is concerned, is counter-Us. If We are going to act, let's be serious. Let's prepare and do, or...

PEACE be with you, Brothers and Sisters, if you are willing to do what is necessary to get it.

16. Mystic Years And Pipe Dreams

Between 1867 and 1877 (100 years ago), at the end of the Civil War, the sun shined bright for Negroes in this country. Negroes were senators, governors, lieutenant-governors, judges and mayors. "Negroes and whites were going to school together, riding on street cars together, and cohabitating..." "A man went to mail a letter, and the postmaster was black. A man committed a crime, and...was arrested by a black policeman, prosecuted by a black solicitor, weighed by a black and white jury and sentenced by a black judge." In many areas of this country, in the 1860s, "men were sampling democracy and finding it to their liking... On hot nights, Negroes and whites walked the wide streets arm in arm and went to (saloons) for a cold drink. The social life was gay, glittering and interracial. A dashing young militia captain gave a ball and Negroes and whites...glided across the polished floor. At official balls, receptions and dinners, Negroes and whites sat down together and got up in peace...There was a mixture of black and white, male and female...Social equality was at its highest pitch."

This was almost freedom. Almost because the recently "freed" slaves realized that freedom was not freedom without a firm economic foundation. They realized that a firm economic foundation was impossible without political power. The ballot and manhood, and forty acres of land, a mule, and treatment due a human being were what the Negro wanted. Neither of these was acceptable in the eyes of most Americans. Social equality for the Black man, maybe; but economic and political power for those same people—NO WAY!!!

But "those damned niggers" kept on demanding them. As a result, and to put the Black man back "in his place", "the white population organized for war. The Negro population, at the same time, was systematically disarmed. By hook and crook, on any and every pretext (excuse), the homes of Negroes were searched and arms were systematically appropriated (taken). Adroitly (expertly) playing on the fears of white governors, who dreaded a race war, Democrats succeeded in disarming or emasculating the Negro militia."

W.E.B. DuBois has called the years between 1867 and 1877 "mystic

BLACK-SMART

years". They were mystic because there was something unreal, insubstantial, about them. Black People were "living the life", but "the life" of the Blacks was not based on Black strengths or Black powers. It was based on international public opinion, American public opinion, the Supreme Court and Congress, etc. The international voices stopped crying out for the Negro because they had to take time to rob and oppress the Blacks who had been left in Africa. American public voices stopped crying for the Negro when Americans got tired of hearing about his problems and realized that, once again, they must devote their time to making money. Congressmen "tricked" the Negro in the presidential election of 1876 and the Supreme Court re-interpreted the law in a manner which excluded the Blacks. Like a pleasant dream the "mystic years" faded away and left Black People unprepared to deal with the reality of white attempts to rid this land of Black People (by whatever means necessary), hopefully, one white editor wrote, "by the 1920s".

We remind you of these event, Brothers and Sisters, because many of you seem to think that the recent years of "progress" (the late 1960s and early 1970s) were unmistakable steps forward for Black People in this country. Many of you never would have thought that, 100 years before, Black People were experiencing the same types of heavenly illusions that many of Us experience today. Blacks are everywhere, holding all types of positions, you say, and making lots of money for the first time. We are on the way up, you say, there is no doubt about that.

Well, there are some doubts, Brothers and Sisters, a whole lot of them. We are not on Our way up. If anything, Our present condition is proof of that. Our recent "strides" prove that We are still being taken through historical cycles by those people who assert themselves and make history. It proves that, woefully, instead of Us making history We are still allowing history to make Us.

Why did history make Us after 1877, People? Because We never looked to Ourselves as a source of political power from which We could effectively form an economic base. We always looked to something other than Us. We failed to realize that things other than Us will desert Us quicker than We will desert Ourselves. Those things deserted Us in the 1870s and, because We were not prepared to stand for Ourselves, We fell.

Brace yourself, Brothers and Sisters, especially you "love" freaks of today who try to convince Us and others (including yourself) that America is frantically trying to create a society which will serve all men, of whatever color. Brace yourself for a crash landing because the same basic circumstances which were present in the 1870s are present today. Every attempt is being made to disarm Us, while whites organize for battle (under the guise of the National Rifle Association, for example). We are sleeping in black and white sheets, with black and white bodies; and We are holding elected offices and getting high post appointments. And We are seeking an economic base and political power. Quite in line with all of this is the fact that We are not looking toward Us as a source of that political power. We are not looking toward Us as a source of political power from which We can effectively form an economic base. We are not looking toward Us to support Us. We are looking for support from others, others who do not care as much for Our well-being as We do. During the late 1960s and early 1970, We forced those "others" to take note of Our plight, to adopt Our cause. Now they are realizing that the adoption is requiring too many of their resources. So, they are taking away their support. They are leaving Us on Our own. Because We have not realized where Our source of power is, We will not be able to support Ourselves. We will not be able to make history, therefore history will make Us. If We don't make some adjustments quickly, Brothers and Sisters, We are going to fall again, and this time We will have no one to blame but Ourselves. We will have no one to blame but Ourselves.

PEACE be with you, Brothers and Sisters, if you are willing to do what is necessary to get it.

BLACK-SMART

17. Know Your Enemies

In order to avoid alliances which will not benefit Black People, three things should be repeated here (especially to you "black and white together" singers and "working class" "communists" and "socialists").

Number one: <u>Racism</u> permeates American society. Because of this, integration is out of the question (it takes two to integrate). But, equality is well within Our reach. We don't need the cooperation of anyone to get equality. We don't need to transform white society in order to get equality. We don't need to rely on Congress and the courts in order to get equality. All We need in order to get equality is Us! Us, as thinking people who plan and act with Us in mind. That's all We need. And, since equality is more desirable than integration (nations have equality), equality is what We should seek.*

Number two: The entire history of the labor-trade union movement has been characterized by racism, manipulation of African workers, and cooperation and collaboration between labor "leaders" and the capitalist class. Not one time in the history of class struggle have Black People been genuinely viewed as oppressed comrades by whites. Blacks have always been viewed as a separate group which can be used to highlight inhumane conditions, but ignored and sacrificed once the bargaining begins. Our relief has never been taken seriously because the whole system of making money and getting over (call it capitalism or anything you like) is based upon the unfair use of Black/African labor and Black/African minerals (land). What the "class strugglers" bargain over is a more equal distribution of the goodies among more white people, with selected provisions for certain brainwashed Negroes who accept the proposition that integration is a necessary first step toward revolutionary progress.

Number three: The long arm of American imperialism results in a tremendous flow of income into this country. This income not only provides the ruling classes with a high standard of living, it provides the working class (whites) with a comfortable standard of living as well. It provides the working class with a standard of living which the working class will refuse to give

BLACK-SMART   53

up. They don't want to destroy the source of their comfort, all they want is a higher degree of comfort. They don't want to destroy imperialism (despite what many of them say to the contrary—their comfort depends on imperialism), therefore they don't want to end the economic enslavement of Black People (in Africa and elsewhere). All they want is a higher standard of living, and they are willing to use and abuse Black People, Brown people, Yellow people and Martians to get it; preferably through the bargaining table, but through what they call "revolution" if all else fails.

What they call revolution cannot be equated to universal progress, Brothers and Sisters. What they call revolution is a change in who holds the privileged positions on the totem pole; it is not the destruction of the totem pole itself. Think about what that means for Black People, then determine if you want to use your energies and intelligence to elevate whites, or if you want to use those energies and intelligence to prepare Blacks for a humanitarian struggle. The choice is Ours to make, Brothers and Sisters. Each of Us should choose wisely.

Peace be with you, Brothers and Sisters, if you are willing to do what is necessary to get it.

*NOTE: We feel it is necessary to define equality, since many Black persons seem incapable of understanding terms and creating definitions which do not begin with or give special consideration to white people.

Equality is the right to control those institutions which affect Our lives and determine Our future. It is the right to determine how Our schools are run and what is taught in them. It is the right to establish a social and economic structure that fits Our views concerning production, distribution and general welfare. It is the right to be self-determining; the right to decide if We should pay taxes and, if so, how they should be spent. It is the right to establish a system of relationships which will be beneficial to Us, Black People. Equality has nothing to do with keeping up with whitey, individually or collectively. It has everything to do with Our natural rights, from the right to withdraw because of individual preferences to the right to join Our forces,

54   BLACK-SMART

claim land which is due Us, and establish a government which will justly represent Our cause at the conference table of nations. That is equality, Brothers and Sisters. Nothing less will do!

PEACE be with you, Brothers and Sisters, if you are willing to do what is necessary to get it.

18. Shotguns Disguised As Ministers

Why is it so difficult to instill pride in Black People today? Because We don't know who Our leaders and heroes were yesterday. Why don't We know? Partly because nearly all of them had a European or Arabic name attached to their African bodies. Why? Because nearly all of them had adopted Christianity or Islam as a religion of expediency, or were forced to carry Christian or Islamic names as a result of enslavement.

Why is it going to be so difficult to instill pride in Black People in the future, say 300 years from now? Because future Blacks are not going to know who their leaders were today. And why wont they know? Because nearly all of Us have Christian or Arabic/Islamic names attached to Our Black bodies. A Black child 300 years from now will say, "White people have names like Martin Luther King, Jr., and think, therefore, that King was probably white. Another Black child will say that Malcolm X was an Arab because Black People don't have a name like El Hagg Malik El Shabazz. Can you imagine that? Three hundred years from now Malcolm X might be identified as an Arab instead of a Black man simply because he innocently embraced a religion to replace the one which had been robbed from him.

Malcolm's original religion, that of Mother Africa, was destroyed by the very Arabs and Christians who, today, will not allow Blacks to adapt their religion without also adapting one of their names. Why is this name change so important? Because to eastern whites (Arabs) and western whites (Europeans/Americans), religion is a political tool used to subdue and eliminate a different group of people as a historical and sociological reality/factor.

Of all the peoples on the face of the earth, none are more naturally spiritual and religious than Black People. Religion is that force which drives all of Nature's parts toward spiritual and physical harmony. Its purpose is to make us freer and more loving, and in traditional Africa it was represented by One Supreme God. It determined how Blacks acted toward one another on social, economic and political levels. Islam and Christianity, on the other hand, are religious ideologies which represent cultures that are dominated by economics and politics. Everything, including religion, revolves around efforts to make money, get land and dominate others. Though they preach love and freedom, they practice deceit and enslavement; and history and their emphasis on how converts identify themselves are proof of this.

Black People's general condition and natural inclinations force many of Us to reach out for some type of religious structure to help Us order Our lives. This is understandable. What needs to be understood, however, is that We don't need to adapt a foreign religious structure at any cost. Convert to Islam, if you will, or to Christianity; but insist that you be allowed to maintain your Blackness (adapt an African name, e.g.). If religion is their main concern, then you will be allowed to do so without any sweat. If, however, they insist that you assume one of their names, for example, then you should realize that religion is not their main concern; and if religion isn't their main concern, then Brothers and Sisters, you/We don't need it (whatever they're offering).

The purpose of this essay is to get Us to realize how We many times innocently surrender vital parts of Our heritage (names, languages, etc.) without realizing how important they are to the future development of all peoples, particularly Blacks. In Our eagerness to relieve Our personal problems We too often look toward other people for solutions and end up accepting or imitating their way of life, their values. We must stop doing this. When We adapt the ways of others, We at the same time give up much that is a part of Ourselves.

This is not an attack on Allah; it is not an attack on God. It is a warning to all of Us to beware of political servants, be they individuals or organizations, which are disguised as religions (or a number of other things). The Almighty isn't concerned about what your name is—political representatives are.

So beware of shotguns disguised as ministers, Brothers and Sisters, and remember that the Almighty does not require you to attend a church, a temple or a mosque in order to get some religious order in your life.

BLACK-SMART   57

19. We Do Not Value Ourselves

We don't strive for or accept those qualities which are good for Our
personal well-being, therefore We find it difficult to get together and build
a way of life, a functional system of values, which will benefit Us socially.

Our experiences in America seem to have left Us unable to choose those
things which are good for Us Brothers and Sisters. Even in cases where Our
personal well-being is involved, We all too often overlook and ignore those
qualities which have evidenced their concern or have proven their worth and
benefit, and instead seek something We would prefer to have (an eye pleaser,
a physical satisfaction, e.g.), or something that calls for less responsibility on
Our part. This is a serious symptom because it indicates that We, individually
and collectively, do not value Ourselves. America's institutions have taught
Us to feel this way! As a result, We don't seek what is good for Us in life
(values, e.g.); all We seek is what We need to "get by" with. Each of Us
realizes, consciously or subconsciously, that by choosing to just "get by", We
eliminate having to critically think about issues and decisions (and Our
responses to them), and We eliminate the need to care about the long range
results of issues and decisions (because future generations will "get by" on
their own, right?).

Evidence from recent history and the present indicate that the majority of
Black People don't care about themselves (America's institutions have done
a good job). Yet, Black People want to break away from the stranglehold of
this mad/white system. How do We propose to do it? What is going to happen
to transform the masses of Black People from non-carers to long range
planners?

Institutions are going to happen Brothers and Sisters—We are going to
become long range planners and achievers—because institutions are the only
vehicles which can affect large, scattered numbers simultaneously. And, since

BLACK-SMART

so many of Us are not in a social frame of mind which will allow Us to build solid structures, it is necessary that each of Us who claims to be progressive take the entire weight until those others begin to follow his/her example and play their proper roles. It is necessary that each of Us who claims to be progressive lay the groundwork for the later development of these institutions. No matter what the price, regardless of the burden, those of Us who claim to be progressive must act accordingly. This is what Rap Brown, C.L.R. James and Barbara Sizemore have been doing. This is what Marcus Garvey, W.E.B. DuBois and Harriet Tubman did. The same is true of Sojourner Truth, Nat Turner, Denmark Veazey, Gabriel Prosser and thousands of others whose names are unknown. The same must be true of the strong among Us today, because the strong can resist the call of the wild and keep the ideas alive which will inspire all of Us to build when We are able to.

Strong institutions do not just pop up, Brothers and Sisters. They are planted, they are nourished, they grow and they are cultivated. Those of Us who are drunk from America's brainwashing aren't in a state of existence to plant. Many wont be able to contribute to the nourishment. The sober among Us must take on those responsibilities. If properly done, all of Us should be able to participate in the growing and cultivating processes. All of Us will be needed.

PEACE be with you, Brothers and Sisters, if you are willing to do what is necessary to get it.

20. Hard To Gain, Easy To Lose

What it took Mao and his comrades more than 50 years to build has been effectively undermined in less than 12 months. What should We, Black People, learn from this experience?

We should recognize, first and foremost, that the Chinese masses allowed this change to take place. They probably didn't want the change but allowed it because they didn't know how to go about getting what they wanted. They planted the seeds for this set of events years earlier when they, the masses, chose to <u>follow</u> Mao instead of trying to understand what he was trying to do and/or how he was trying to do it. They grabbed onto the man, and said "later" for the understanding. Now they are leaderless and troubled because the man is dead and the understanding was rejected.

We are not attempting to be unfair to any mass of people, Brothers and Sisters. By nature the overwhelming majority of most people are non-political, because politics is not a natural concern. Politics is a scheme of man; unfortunately it has developed into a factor which cannot be ignored even by those who only want to eat, dress and take shelter. It has become a dominant force in each person's life, therefore each person should take the time necessary to become adequately versed in its processes. It is nice to put your faith in leaders, but we can't think of even one leader who came here and got away without dying (while life goes on). Each of Us, instead, must understand what Our leaders understand and thereby be able to do what needs to be done regardless of his/her presence or absence.

(We should also be constantly mindful of the historical fact that it is much more difficult to maintain a function which benefits the masses and depends upon the masses for continued success than it is to maintain a function which will benefit a select few. This is true because masses—large numbers—have a slower adjustment rate than small numbers. If an institution which benefits the masses shakes, the masses suffer tremendously; if an institution which benefits a select few shakes, that group can make a quick adjustment which might reduce the impact of the malfunction. This does not mean, however, that it is better to let the institutions benefit a select few. Quite to the contrary, it is the reason why the masses should be completely involved in the institution-making process.)

Secondly, We should recognize that the same forces which undermined Mao and the Chinese community are already thriving in the Black community (We are in the heart of the capitalist world and must be constantly mindful of this fact's influence on Us when We evaluate Ourselves. Under no circumstances should We rate Ourselves "progressive" if, in fact, We are not, because it will hinder the development of all Black People). Those forces are represented by individuals and groups that have a surface concern for the plight of the masses but a deep concern that they be allowed to seek recognition and compensation for their individual/group achievements and initiative. One can easily spot such representatives in establishment roles (a thriving young businessman, an ambitious lawyer or clerk), but it is not so easy to spot such representatives in non-establishment roles. They are there though, and they are flourishing. Check out the "community" organizations whose membership is exclusive, individuals who look for a "pat on the back", or either one of them which counts its dollars and cents in terms of its survival and not in terms of the community's survival or benefit. Check them out Brothers and Sisters, and watch them closely. Once Blacks attempt to establish procedures and limitations (a system) which seek to benefit the masses, the fakes will attempt to overthrow those procedures and limitations because individual recognition and compensation is MOST important to them.

We must be careful, We must be very careful, if We want the masses (all of Us) to progress. And We must be just as sincere. Which means, We have to work with the masses not to get the masses to follow us, but to inspire the masses to become self-determining and self-propelling. We must seek mass participation, mass understanding and mass leadership. If any of you revolutionaries think that these are impossible aims, then you might as well hang up your revolutionary rhetoric. History has repeatedly (and recently) demonstrated that nothing less will do.

21. The Challenge

Watchin

      Waitin

            Lookin

What's gonna happen?

to me

      to Us

           to the world .

What could happen?

Black People could break bad—

                                  but they wont.

Will anybody?

         break bad

Will anybody?

         break wrong's back

         Or

Will everybody?

         be

Watchin

      Waitin

           and

Lookin

The poem lays it on the line, Brothers and Sisters. It doesn't specifically mention but one group of people, Black People; and it says We definitely wont do anything to bring about any changes. Let's prove the poem a lie. Let's prove that We are men and women who will no longer stand for the butchery of Our freedom. Let's prove that We are men and women who will no longer

           BLACK-SMART

leave Our salvation in the hands of people who are not inclined to act human. Let's prove that We are tired of "watchin, waitin, and lookin" for a hole to appear which We can crawl into for safety. Let's prove that We have reached the point where We are ready to build Our own "hole", one which will represent Black People as a Black nation. Let's work for Our nation, a Republic of New Afrika, and prepare a future for Our children which will make them proud of Us.

PEACE be with you, Brothers and Sisters, if you are willing to do what is necessary to get it.

BLACK
Section Two
SMART

BLACK-SMART:
SHORT ESSAYS TOWARD PROGRESS

VOLUME 2

TABLE OF ESSAYS

21. The Challenge

Watchin

      Waitin

           Lookin

What's gonna happen?

to me

      to Us

           to the world .

What <u>could</u> happen?

Black People could break bad—

                    but they wont.

Will anybody?

        break bad

Will anybody?

        break wrong's back

        Or

Will everybody?

      be

Watchin

      Waitin

        and

Lookin

The poem lays it on the line, Brothers and Sisters. It doesn't specifically mention but one group of people, Black People; and it says We definitely wont do anything to bring about any changes. Let's prove the poem a lie. Let's prove that We are men and women who will no longer stand for the butchery of Our freedom. Let's prove that We are men and women who will no longer leave Our salvation in the hands of people who are not inclined to act human. Let's prove that We are tired of "watchin, waitin, and lookin" for a hole to appear which We can crawl into for safety. Let's prove that We have reached the point where We are ready to build Our own "hole", one which will represent Black People as a Black nation. Let's work for Our nation, a Republic of New Afrika, and prepare a future for Our children which will make them proud of Us.

PEACE be with you, Brothers and Sisters, if you are willing to do what is necessary to get it.

22. "The Ape That Tricked Black People"

Brothers and Sisters, history has demonstrated that nothing which benefits the masses can revolve around a handful of individuals and last. Therefore, it is of the greatest importance that We stop viewing history from the standpoint of what certain men did, and view it instead from the standpoint of how the masses acted and benefited, or how the masses failed to act and allowed themselves to be exploited. Such an interpretation would result in the common man recognizing how important he/she is to the historical process, and simultaneously begin to destroy the myth of the "great" man who is able to accomplish things which the "ordinary" man is incapable of accomplishing. This is critical to Black People because We are confronted by a problem whose solution lies in mass participation. We cannot afford to have some of Us feeling that, because of the size and scope of the problem, he or she is incapable of contributing to its elimination.

What does history (as We know it) tell people? It tells people to follow the examples set by Napoleon Bonaparte, William Pitt, George Washington, Thomas Jefferson and Henry Kissinger. What did these men do? They got an understanding of what was going on and entered the struggle on the side of those who exploit the masses. They helped a group of exploiters maintain their domination of the masses of the people. Why were they successful? Was it because of their extraordinary genius or extraordinary organizing abilities? No. It was because of the ignorance and lack of assertiveness of the masses. When the ordinary man and woman did assert themselves, the exploiters could do nothing but wait until they tired. This is revealed even in the most prejudiced (exploiter-oriented) history books. Let Us review a couple of cases.

Napoleon Bonaparte has been called one of the greatest white men of all time because of his military genius and because he stabilized the rule of the exploiters in France during the late 1790s and early 1800s. But what did his greatness depend upon? It depended upon the ignorance and lack of organized resistance of the masses. The men who fought in his army were ignorant of the fact that he was using them to exploit their sisters and brothers. If they had realized this they would not have fought for him; he would have been powerless. Therefore, what he is given credit for accomplishing was actually accomplished by a segment of the masses - ordinary men and women. Likewise, why was Napoleon able to stabilize the rule of the exploiters in France? Because the masses of the people there had tired of hitting the streets. They had rebelled on a spurt of emotions, and emotions are not enough to destroy exploitation. Their lack of organized revolt and planning allowed Napoleon to take advantage of them in the long run, and he did. Not because he was great, but because ordinary men and women were not prepared to constantly resist him. They stopped resisting, they joined his forces, Napoleon succeeded. Napoleon himself was powerless to do anything! One man or a handful of men is always powerless, Brothers and Sisters, unless you do what is necessary to make him powerful (act for him or fail to act against him).

What could William Pitt do when the British people opposed him? Nothing. What could George Washington do when the men who fought for him deserted him? Nothing. What could Henry Kissinger do in Lebanon? Nothing. The people there said "later for him." What happened to Richard Nixon's power when the American people jumped against him? It vanished. It always has been the case, it always will be the case. The ordinary man and woman, by what they do or fail to do as a group of people, make history, Brothers and Sisters, not individuals or small groups of persons.

What else does history (as We know it) tell people? It tells people how to act if they get an understanding of what is going on but choose to not enter the struggle on the side of the exploiters. It tells them to act in a manner that will not destroy the exploiters. It tells them to display their knowledge, to let everyone know how smart they are or how well they can debate. It even encourages persons (who insist) to stand on a platform and tell the masses, in one hour, what is happening and what needs to be done. It does not encourage people to use violence when violence is needed and, even more important, it does not encourage persons who understand to go among the masses and provide them with the knowledge and understanding they need to

BLACK-SMART

free themselves and maintain their freedom.

This is critical to an understanding of why many people-oriented movements fail. Their leaders, instead of seeking to revolve the movement around the people, become the movement themselves. Their relationship with the people is "Follow me, I will set you free." After a while the leaders die; with their death the movement falters because the masses do not have the understanding their leaders had.

Why is this understanding so important. Because understanding leads Us to the realization that difficult problems will not crumble if We huff and puff. Understanding guides Us and prepares Us to deal with problems within the context of time; it teaches Us that problems which have been around for a long period of time are not going to be solved in a month or two. Understanding, therefore, realizes the ineffectiveness of attempting to deal with exploitation with emotional outbursts, and teaches that organization, planning, mass participation and persistence are the keys to historical developments that will benefit people (masses), not just persons.

According to certain versions of history, the masses only exist at times, therefore it is not conceivable that they are important to the historical process. It is even less conceivable that they are capable of dealing with the problems that confront them. There is a tendency, then, to ignore the masses. There is a tendency to take it for granted that they cannot think, understand nor act intelligently. **We must never feel this way about the masses of Black People! We must not have the masses of Black People believing that they are historical zeroes!! But many already do. Why??**

For years Black historians aped the manner of Our exploiters when telling Us the story of history (white developments). We developed a "great man" complex; We began to think that only a "great white father" could help Us. Lately, these same Black historians have been telling Us Our history in the same way. They have, in fact, told Black People that a messiah (Booker T. Washington, Martin Luther King, Jr., Malcolm X, etc.) comes along at certain times who deals with the problems the average man is incapable of dealing with. This messiah, they imply, because of his exceptional qualities and abilities, is able to control the actions of thousands, even millions of persons. This is ridiculous (no one controls more than one person— himself), but it is accepted by many persons who, on the whole, do not attempt to deal with Our problems as a social/group question. They instead strike out against the injustices they suffer with individual bursts of rebellion. They concern themselves with the little *effects* of the problem that causes them to suffer, but feel incapable of dealing with the problem itself. They have the "I/You can't change the world" attitude because they have been convinced that only "great" men can bring about processes that "change the world." This is beneficial to Our exploiters because the basis of their power over Us is the failure of Us, Black People, to act as a group. As long as We rebel individually or wait for the timely appearance of a messiah they can continue to take advantage of Us.

We cannot afford to have any of Us feeling that what he or she does is unimportant from the standpoint of historical developments. We cannot afford to have any of Us feeling that some other person is the key to changing Our conditions. Each of Us must feel that the key to Black progress is his/her participation, and act accordingly. A proper interpretation of history will help such a frame of mind develop because it will reveal that the ordinary man and woman has always been the major factor in all historical developments.

So, We must start telling the story of history from the standpoint of the masses. [Two slave revolts, one led by Gabriel Prosser and the other led by Denmark Vesey, failed because some slaves failed to keep their mouths shut. David Walker's Appeal was so important because so many slaves were plotting against their masters after hearing about it. Henry Highland Garnet was recognized because so many slaves were running from the plantation. Harriet Tubman was so effective because none of the slaves betrayed her. The Emancipation Proclamation was issued because the North needed Black fighters to win the Civil War. Marcus Garvey was effective because of the support he received from the masses. Malcolm X and Martin Luther King were effective because of the support they received from the masses. And so on]. We must convince the man on the street that his involvement in group

74

activities or his failure to get involved in group activities will determine the quality of his personal life. We must convince ordinary persons that this has always been the case; that no man is great unless the masses make him great, that no man can effectively deal with a social problem unless the masses give him the power to do so.

This is a gigantic task, Brothers and Sisters, but necessity demands not one bit less (We are confronted by a gigantic problem). So We must start attacking it, all/each of Us. At this moment you can help change Our future by passing this information on to buddies, classmates, schoolteachers and college professors, etc. Talk to people and stress to them the importance of this interpretation to the development of Black People. Stress to them that it is not enough to imply what the masses are responsible for— it must be stated clearly and forcefully. Stress to them how important their response is to this realization, and make them aware of the role they and you have to play. Let them know what their people and progress demands of them, and urge them to meet those demands.

Black liberation/Black self-determination is no easy task, Brothers and sisters. Don't look for an easy way out—— there isn't one.

PEACE be with you, Brothers and Sisters, if you are willing to do what is necessary to get it.

23. "Stages of Individual Development"

Revolution is a process, Brothers and Sisters. It involves stages of individual development and stages of social/group development which could determine whether We succeed in Our endeavors or fail to succeed. Here are some of the stages We have to realize as We strive toward the re-emergence of Black People in Our proper place in the natural order of life.

Individually;

We have to stop criticizing other people, especially white people, for what they attempt to do to harm Us. Whether We progress or suffer over an extended period of time will be determined by what We, Black People, do or fail to do.

We need a change of attitude toward each other. We need to begin to respect Black People. Each of Us needs to be positive with Our Sisters and Brothers, even if it runs the risk of a personal loss or inconvenience. We also need to re-evaluate Our priorities. This will eliminate a lot of the bull-jiving and petty-mindedness which seem to characterize Our life-style and prepare Us to let principles (basic social values) determine what We do. If We let Our principles motivate Us We are not likely to get turned off when Our positive efforts are not fully appreciated by those We attempt to assist.

Everything We read, everything we see and everything We hear should be carefully analyzed by each of Us. That way, newspapers, radio shows and tv news reports are less likely to mislead Us. We cannot trust those who presently control these facilities to tell Us the truth, so it is important that each of Us be able to recognize an untruth for what it is. Additionally, as We begin to analyze materials, each of Us will develop the habit of doing his/her own thinking. This is necessary.

Institutions are the only vehicles which can affect large, scattered numbers simultaneously (at the same time). Institutions are the plans which will prepare Us for freedom. Until those institutions evolve and become a dominating force, each of Us who claims to be progressive, each of Us who claims to want a change must take the full responsibility for laying the groundwork for that change if necessary. We must discipline Ourselves and steer Ourselves toward a revolutionary frame of mind until institutions begin to dominate which encourage mass revolutionary development.

Finally, and very important, each of Us must adhere to the doctrine that the people are the source of power; under no circumstance should any of Us look elsewhere for power. We must make Black People aware of Our power by being positively aggressive, historically aware and knowledgeable of economic and political concepts of survival and government.

Collectively;

We have proven that We can overcome all obstacles and act like other people want Us to act. What We have failed to prove is that We can establish a social, economic and governmental order based upon Our tendencies, Our values, Our priorities. This We must do. We have to act for a change. We have to take some cold, analytical looks at Black People, determine what We must do and develop institutions that will enable Us to do it. This will reduce Our tendency to respond or react, and thereby decrease the power structure's ability to manipulate Us. Additionally, as We act, Our young will learn to act— they will learn to be positively aggressive.

Similarly, We need to demonstrate Our will to be Us by not tacitly/ indirectly demonstrating that We want to be a part of some other group. We must not accept other people's priorities. This will necessarily involve a degree of political awareness and involvement. This does not mean that We must register and vote; it means that We have to know what to do to control those factors which determine the quality of Our life— as they are influenced by other people, but mostly as they are influenced by Us.

To be effective, We have to have a clear understanding of where We want to go. But knowing where We want to go is no good if conditions do not exist which will enable Us to get there. In Our case, the case of Black People, these conditions (positive attitudes, initiative, perseverance, etc.) have to be cultivated. Then We can bring about some tangible changes.

PEACE be with you, Brothers and Sisters, if you are willing to do what is necessary to get it.

24. "Roots"

When We discuss *Roots* or think about it, We should not let Our thoughts be confined to a tv presentation. We should view *Roots* as an education, one which, compared to most classroom experiences of today, is indeed revealing. We should also view it as a message, one that got across to 30 million Black persons at the same time. However, We must not forget that it was televised by a power structure which only does things that will benefit it. Why it decided to televise *Roots*, other than for economic reasons, is debatable. What is certain though, is that Black People should not evaluate the message(s) in the tv presentation unless We are aware of four historical facts.

Number One: Islam is not the indigenous/original African religion (the tv presentation would lead people to think it is). Quite to the contrary, Islam was used to help destroy the religious references of the African People. Islam was used by Arabs (eastern whites) in Africa from the 7th century on just as Christianity was used by Europeans (western whites) in Africa after 1400— to enslave the Black man and take his land. **The African People fought against Islam for centuries;** some clans tired of the constant instability caused by resisting and submitted to Islam (Kunta Kinte's is probably an example). It was not because Islam was their preference, but because submitting to Islam guaranteed their existence.

Number Two: Slavery was/is no isolated event. Slavery was not something that white people accidentally did and it is not an unusual thing for them to do. Slavery was a nightmare, a living hell white people **planned** for Black People so they, white people, could make money, just like lynchings and burnings were planned by white people to keep Black People from gaining political power. Slavery was planned just like the attempts to wipe out Indians in this country were planned [whites call it "how the West was won"], and for the same economic reasons. Slavery was planned just like the Ku Klux Klan was planned; just like dropping bombs on people is planned; just like hunger, poverty and slums are planned; just like the attempted destruction of Vietnam was planned; just like the experiments with syphilis on 600 Black men in Alabama and the sterilizing of those Black girls in Mississippi were planned; just like killing Black leaders and destroying Black organizations like the Black Panther Party is planned; and just like white people plan hundreds of other atrocities on non-white peoples annually. Please don't forget this, Brothers and Sisters. Whites have always plotted in the past, they are plotting now and they are going to be plotting in the future. Don't think a tv presentation of *Roots* has changed or will change their conduct.

Number Three: There are some whites out there who are okay, but don't take it for granted that your "friend" is one of them. As a matter of fact, to be safe you should assume that you are not going to run into one that is okay. Whether you run into one who you think is okay or not, don't base your course of action upon that one's sincerity. If you have a rule (Black People can't trust white people), and an exception to the rule (some whites are okay), prepare yourself according to the rule and let the exceptions take care of themselves.

Number Four: The Negro's progress, when compared with the hell of slavery and the extremely vicious racism of Jim Crow (segregation), has been startling; but when compared to the progress of other minorities (especially white minorities) it is shameful. Black People have never received a fair deal from this country. We have made some progress, but most of what We think is progress is an illusion because **We do not have any power.** We have never had any power, and We should not expect those who control this country to give Us any. So don't get the impression, after watching *Roots* and comparing the times then with the times now, that We have a lot to be thankful for. Don't think that America has been giving Us Our due after all. Don't think that, because We are still last hired and first fired, We still die "in disproportionate numbers", We are still forced to live on welfare pennies, We still populate the worst areas of the country, etc. In short, We are still not allowed to live as human beings should live, and We are still not given the respect and consideration which are due all humans. We are still exploited, misused, abused and discarded.

Think about these factors constantly, Brothers and Sisters. Don't let these people get you to thinking things that are going to interfere with your tendency to act intelligently. Don't let those people subconsciously brainwash you.

PEACE be with you, Brothers and Sisters, if you are willing to do what is necessary to get it.

25. "African Socialism"

We are going to take this opportunity to introduce the concept of African Socialism to the readers of "The People's Newsletter." Just like any other form of socialism, the apparent focus of African Socialism revolves around the popular/mass distribution of wealth which a nation produces. It involves questions such as the common man's access to such wealth as food, clothing, shelter, medical attention, education, security, mobility and other tangible and intangible realities that make life livable. However, there is a basic difference between African Socialism and what Europeans (white people) call socialism, a difference so basic that it questions whether European socialism(s) is really social. The difference revolves around the *attitude* people take on the question of economics. Whereas European socialists view mass economic prosperity as a key to human survival, African Socialism views human survival and concern as the key to mass economic prosperity. In other words, where Europeans view a class struggle as the key to the creation of a socialist state, African Socialism views concern for the human being as that key.

This is not intended as a declaration that class consciousness, in any society, is a negligible factor. Instead, it recognizes the fact that true concern for human beings cannot be developed under a train of thought which centers around a non-human factor (like monetary income). The core of a *social* train of thought must be concern for human beings; education and common sense, as expressed in official policies, will dictate that all persons must have access to those tangible and intangible realities which make the human's life worth living.

But economic prosperity must not be Our aim; concern for Our People must be. For this reason much of "The People's Newsletter" has been devoted to urging individuals to go through changes that will eventually be of gigantic importance to Black People. We have urged people to make personal sacrifices, to practice self-discipline, self-control and general respect, and to understand

basic principles which govern life and interpersonal relationships. We have urged these things because we want to help create a socialist *attitude* among as many of Our people as we can at this stage of Our development. This attitude can keep capitalist concepts from interfering with Our goals at this, a developmental stage, and at later stages of Our drive toward self-determination. And, just as important, this attitude can help defeat class-consciousness if it appears among Us as an independent people.

This philosophy, as it relates to Black People in America, recognizes two important factors. It recognizes that all of Us are not going to adopt this frame of mind, but that an early Black socialist State can be composed of those who are able to do so. [By early, we mean right now. Those of Us with the proper attitude can function as African socialists right now.] Secondly, it recognizes that there is more to a revolution than confrontations and more to a nation than land and governments. Since a declared confrontation is not presently at hand, and since We are still undecided as to where Our nation will take its physical form, We should deal with an issue which will always be at hand. That issue is the attitude of Our People toward each other and Our attitudes toward the processes which should determine Our official policies. Once the people are firm and committed to a course of action in that area (the attitude area), the other questions will be resolved by Our determination to get that which is due Us.

So, African Socialism is Our key, Brothers and Sisters. It does not say that We are not going to have to take matters to an extreme level, it says the basis of Our extremities will be Our concern for Our Brothers and Sisters. How are We going to develop this necessary concern for Black People (that many prefer to ignore)? We are going to start off on very small scales and expand those scales to cover more of Our population. Each of Us should sacrifice for and share with Our family, Our extended family, individuals in the community and organizations which you deem are beneficial (by Our standards) to Our community. It is a difficult formula to follow because there are no institutions presently functioning which constantly urge Us to do these

things. But We must do them until We are close enough to each other to plan other measures.

Don't tell us that this simple sounding plan cannot work because persons are not going to follow it, tell us what each person can do to make it a success. Tell us how We can overcome all forces that will certainly attempt to keep Our plan from working.

PEACE be with you, Brothers and Sisters, if you are willing to do what is necessary to get it.

26. "The People's Newsletter"

Various individuals have approached us concerning *The People's Newsletter*. We feel that the community at large might be interested in some of our responses.

(A) We are not writing about a Black fantasy land in *The People's Newsletter*. The suggestions we make concerning Black persons' attitudes toward and respect for other Blacks is not intended to bring about an "if Black People were only like this" response. It is intended to get you to check yourself out and recognize what changes you need to go through in order to be a positive force and example for other Black persons. We are not appealing to "iffers" or dreamers; we are appealing to persons who can (1) realize that they are part of the problem and (2) bring about those necessary personal changes that will eliminate or effectively control that part of them which helps keep the Black race on the bottom.

(B) Several editions of *The People's Newsletter* will overlap in places. This is intentionally done. We do not feel that a key to progress is a new idea every month or so. We do feel that a key is getting a thorough understanding and realization of those factors which are basic to Our inertia (lack of productive motion). Since there is an interrelationship between various aspects of Black consciousness and Black awareness, and since many persons forget what was said in one edition just about as soon as they finish reading it (which is unfortunate), we put some of the same messages to them in later editions from a slightly different angle. That way, it is a little more difficult for our readers to lose grasp of the ideas that we feel all of Us should practice and be constantly aware of.

(C) We do not believe we are berating (making fun of) white people just because we appreciate Black People and ideas and values that Black People have been known to live by. We capitalize terms which refer to Black People (We, Our, Us) because the collective is supreme to Us. Likewise, we fail to capitalize that which refers to the singular because it is not deserving of a capital. [For related practices, notice how white people capitalize "I" but fail to capitalize "we." This is because the individual and his aspirations mean more to white people than the collective group and its aspirations/welfare.

(D) *The People* is not trying to encourage individual or isolated acts of rebellion. History has repeatedly revealed that isolated acts do not bring about any noticeable degree of change; they never affect an institution at its core. The only things individual rebellers usually get are a glimpse of glory and a lifetime in jail (maximum confinement).

Our emphasis has never been on destruction, it has been on building. We have not talked about destroying any government; we have only talked about building a social structure (way of-life) that will be proper and beneficial to Black People. However, we insist that Black People have a right to seek a better way-of-life. We also insist that Black People have the right to resist those who attempt to keep Us from doing what We have a right to do.

(E) The written word can be easily misinterpreted, and an idea or thought can be miswritten or confusing. For that reason, *The People* is appreciative of responses it receives from the community. Clarity and understanding are important to all of Us.

PEACE be with you, Brothers and Sisters, if you are willing to do what is necessary to get it.

27. "Let's Redistribute Our Wealth"

Wealth is a material factor, Brothers and Sisters. It is tangible (We can touch it and see it!), and it appears in the form of land, homes, cars, income, clothes, food, and other necessities and conveniences. But wealth is also intangible (though We can't touch it, We can *feel* it). It is positive vibrations, concern for others, etc. It is positive attitudes toward Our potential. In short then, wealth is that activity that gives life its actual or potential "live-ability".

Since wealth makes life worth living, it is important that the masses of Black People in this country share an abundance of one form of wealth and enough of the other form of wealth to maintain Ourselves until We have progressed to the point where We can create a social system which will have as its purpose **Our** maintenance. We need an abundance of the spiritual forms of wealth. We need an abundance of positive vibrations and positive attitudes toward Our ability to do whatever We need to do. But, how can this feeling of confidence in Blackness make itself a dominant force if the majority of Us who have a degree of material wealth refuse to share even a small portion of it with those of Us who do not possess any material wealth? How can the majority of Us feel confident in the ability of Our race to restructure society if members of Our race do not consistently act in a manner which demonstrates that they are willing to make some sacrifices in order to get the opportunity to restructure society and establish a new social system?

Oppressed peoples in all parts of the world are calling for a "redistribution of the wealth." They know that the key to their relief is in the pockets of their oppressors, and to get any relief at all they have to go to their oppressors as either beggars or rebels. But Black People in this country are in a somewhat different position. We don't have to go to Our oppressors for economic relief because We possess enough economic wealth to relieve Our community of much of its economic poverty. **All We need to do is redistribute that wealth which is already among Us.** If We redistribute the material wealth We already have, We will create an abundance of spiritual wealth within Our community. This spiritual wealth will create feelings of community among Blacks and confidence in Blackness that will enable Us to take any additional material wealth that We feel Our community needs in order to thrive.

The material wealth we are referring to is not in the hands of Black millionaires, nor is it in the hands of the "educated" Black middle class. If that were the case, then there would be no practical need in making this proposal because the two groups mentioned are satisfied with the way things are going. The wealth we are referring to, the wealth that can relieve the material needs of Our community, is in the hands of those of Us who constantly criticize and are thoroughly pissed off by a social order that refuses to recognize Our worth. It is among these malcontents, most of whom make less than $7000-$8000 per year, that the material wealth exists that can start Us to moving in a position of power which will enable Us to demand that We be dealt with as equals.

So let's start redistributing that wealth, Brothers and Sisters. Each of Us can start by eliminating a lot of the wasteful activities We engage in that require some of Our wealth. Then We can take that wealth that We once wasted and redistribute it. Each person can redistribute the wealth himself/herself, each person can give what he would like redistributed to an organization and have that organization carry out the task, or a combination of the two processes can function. All those of Us who have will be doing is give what We can spare (funds, clothes, etc.) to those who do not have. However, any time that this happens, anytime wealth is redistributed, it should be made certain that the persons who receive that wealth understand it as a part of a general movement among Black People and not as an isolated, personal or organizational thing. This is critical because it directs those who receive the wealth toward a community frame of thought and helps to eliminate the "that person is all right" response (as opposed to "most Black persons are all right").

African socialism, with its motivating force of human concern, recognizes that the key to Our welfare is Us. It requires that no one should be in control of Our destiny but Us, and that We can only control Our destiny by revolving the heartbeat of Our community around institutions which are peculiarly structured to serve Our needs at a particular stage of development. Our structure must have Our maintenance as its goal. Therefore, it must be a carefully worked out formula which recognizes the uniqueness of Our situation. It cannot be a slightly warped imitation of someone else's structure because someone else's structure was particularly and peculiarly planned to serve that someone else. It must come from Us, from within Ourselves, be created by Us, and revolve around Our strengths. Anything else, even though it might seem a lot better because of its temporary advantages, will be a lot worse because it will leave Us at the mercy of a force which is not controlled by Us.

What we have suggested in this essay is the beginning of an economic structure that can serve Us, Brothers and Sisters. It is a skeleton, a bony structure, but it is based upon the uniqueness of Our situation; and it will grow as We grow and flourish as We discover that it will work if We want it to work. No ifs, no buts, just some assistance please. We'll establish an organization to control its processes and make the necessary adjustments as We stumble and stride toward "developing Blackness."

PEACE be with you, Brothers and Sisters, if you are willing to do what is necessary to get it.

28. "Caucasian Involvement In Black Organizations"

Throughout the publication of *The People's Newsletter*, *The People* has tried to give a conceptual view of all proposals, situations, possibilities, etc. Concepts are important because they provide persons with a basis from which they can make an intelligent decision, and that is what we want you to be able to do. We want you to be able to make an intelligent decision. We don't want you to accept what we say simply because we say it. We want you to accept it because it makes sense. If you feel it does not make sense or is not logical, then you would be doing yourself and Black People in general a disfavor by acting as if it does.

At this time, however, we are going to discuss a resolution we have made concerning *The People* and Caucasians (white people). We are going to do this at the risk of alienating many persons of Our color, and that fact alone should indicate how serious we are on the issue.

There is no place in our organization for white involvement. We don't want any of them to know what Black People are planning to do. We don't even want them to read Black literature. At this stage of the development of Black People, as far as *The People* is concerned, Caucasians need not even exist.

Some might call this a racist position; others will call it counter-revolutionary. We grant that you have the option to call it whatever you want to. However, *we* don't call it a racist position. We call it a practical position that seems to be even more practical in light of the history of white/Black relations in this country. It is practical because it recognizes that We, Black People, need to experience certain processes *alone* if We are going to develop Respect, Confidence and Pride in Our race and its potential. These intangibles are steps toward the self-reliance attitudes which African Socialism always demands. The position becomes even more practical when We get the content of the messages/lessons which history has repeatedly attempted to teach Us. Whites don't give a damn about Our welfare. They don't give a damn about

Our anything! Anytime they appear to adapt Our cause, they do so to either keep Us from taking the extreme measures that should be taken, or to highlight an injustice that slightly cripples some of them (and a lot of Us), or simply because they are afraid to not be aware of what We have on Our minds. The only white person who is an exception to each of these reasons was John Brown, a man who is ridiculed and called mad by the supporters of this power structure and who is ignored by the white "liberals" who quote Malcolm X (for example) today. They don't mind publicizing Black persons who have taken Black People seriously, but they don't want the word to get around that one sane white person has taken Black People seriously as well. So, later for them and their pretensions.

Counter-revolutionary? Not in the least. Our position recognizes that We have to make Ourselves revolutionary before We can present Ourselves as a viable revolutionary force in the world. Those of Us who don't understand this are in need of some assistance and proper direction. Those whites who don't understand it don't understand it because it is not to their advantage to understand it. And anyway, why is it that anything that is not integrated (all-Black) must be counter-revolutionary? Or, put another way, what is it about an integrated movement that makes it necessarily revolutionary? Could the answer to this question lay in brainwashed minds which are only receptive to white definitions of critical terms?

If you are going to tell Us that Blacks and whites have the same enemies, please don't do so. Our enemies are capitalism/imperialism/racism and their manifestations. We don't know what the whites are fighting against, other than Us (check your history). And, even if we did have the same enemies, does that necessarily make us allies or friends? *The People* doesn't think so. People who despise and hate each other can be threatened by the same enemy. Thus, *if* Blacks and whites have the same enemy, We can fight that enemy on Our front and they can fight that enemy on their front. Quite frankly, that is exactly what should be happening.

If some white people are genuinely concerned about the struggle of Black People, let them show that concern by positioning themselves exactly where

We want them to be. That is not in Our community, nor is it in the midst of Our nationalist/revolutionary or protest movement. Presently, they can appropriately position themselves in their own communities or in the revolutionary battlefields of southern Africa (under Black command). If they are not willing to content themselves with either of those assignments, then any assistance they give is more likely to harm Us than help Us.

If you mix coffee with cream you come out with a weak solution. Let the coffee stay black and hot and all of its strength will come through. Malcolm recognized that fifteen years ago, and it is still true today. We should never ignore a truth.

PEACE be with you, Brothers and Sisters, if you are willing to do what is necessary to get it.

29. "Black Dis-Unity," Part 1

Traditionally, Black People have been a very democratically inspired People. Since any practical democratic system must be relatively small to maintain its just and humane nature (as it relates to each individual), the Black democrats subtly developed anti-empire attitudes and practices. They recognized no advantages to submitting the will of a village or tribe or an ethnic group to the will of a large, centralized state government. They recognized, instead, that a state would infringe upon the rights of each group (and thereby, each individual), so they resisted all efforts which had political centralization as their objective.

With the passage of time Blacks began to recognize the military advantages of tribal alliances (racial unity), and a process started which resulted in the creation of huge states (empires) which had a central point of authority. Each tribe or ethnic group theoretically owed allegiance to the central government (they paid taxes, tributes, etc.), but in practice remained nearly unaffected by it unless a matter was being dealt with which threatened the security and survival of the state membership itself. At such times, all of the petty differences would be dismissed and the basic similarities would emerge and cause one solid state image to project itself.

What is being said, Brothers and Sisters, is that Black People, Our Ancestors, who had no real concept of "race", and who had certain ideas which each group considered to be of the utmost importance, were able to lay aside those group ideologies or preferences and unite to a formidable degree on the basis of their color and survival. The question which is repeatedly asked today is, "Why can't Black People in this country, who have a thorough understanding of 'race' and historical knowledge of relations among various races, do likewise?"

The answer lies in Our inability to spit out the foreign ideologies which seem to have entered Our bloodstream. Instead of maintaining Our uniqueness

BLACK-SMART

as the factor around which all of Us rally, We have let some impractical (that which cannot be practiced now) trains of thought convert Us into universal men and women— at a time when those who have power are not the least bit universal. Many of Us, from positions of impotence and without any vehicles operating that can popularize Our ideas and ideals nationally, are calling for a world community of equality among all races while the major factions of other races are promoting "us first and us only" campaigns. The result is that the other races march for themselves and advance to a position from which they can popularize their ideologies, while We march for all mankind and remain in a position of powerlessness, a position which leaves Us incapable of popularizing *any* ideology.

At this time the foreign ideologies which have most prepared Us for extinction/elimination are the ideologies of integration, particularly political integration, and the ideology of religious conversion, particularly to the Islamic "faith". Both of these ideologies seek to convince Us that Our color is no big deal; that the key to power in this world is without racial links. The integrationist ideologies tell Us that all colors have to work together to defeat the powers that oppress all people, that a Black-only ideology will only add fuel to the fire and should therefore not be followed/espoused. The Islamic ideology tells Us to conduct Ourselves according to the dictates of the Koran, which has laid out a master plan that is color blind (if only it were practiced as such!). Many of Us who are politically sensitive, but whose minds are somewhat politically underdeveloped (or over-exploited), grab onto one or the other of these two universal ideologies and hold onto them at the expense of denying the political reality of Our color and the survival of Our race. We absolutely refuse to rally around an ideology of race, and Our race suffers.... evermore, evermore, evermore.

(We specifically speak of Islam in this essay because, over the decades, Blacks who have been converted to Christianity have discovered that they do not have to sacrifice their Blackness in order to be a Christian. Since Islam is relatively a novelty (new) to Us, most of its converts are still somewhat romantic and have therefore not yet arrived at a similar conclusion.)

This essay does not intend to imply that the ideologies mentioned above are the sole causes of Black dis-unity. It only states that foreign influences are the keys to Our dis-unity. Why? Because they represent forces which many Blacks are instinctively opposed to and refuse to join with at any cost. They represent forces which demand an absence of Black self-determination. This is not to say that there are no foggy areas among Us; several such areas do exist, but none that any sincere Black person would fail to dismiss in a time of crisis (like the one that presently confronts Us).

There is a natural tendency among Us to do Our own thing, either individually or organizationally, but there is a deeper tendency among Us to rally as a mass when Our survival is threatened. If We fail to do this, then something has interfered with Our drive to survive. Since the drive to survive is a natural instinct, whatever interferes with it must be of a foreign origin— a foreign element. Among Us, that element must be eliminated.

PEACE be with you, Brothers and Sisters, if you are willing to do what is necessary to get it.

30. "Black Dis-Unity," Part 2

It seems that dis-unity is a tradition with Black People; is even bred into Us. What began thousands of years ago as an undefined but democratic urge to "do Our own thing" as small, family-based groups which were not antagonistic toward one another developed, as a result of Our contact with the horrors of invasion, slavery and the slave trade (as introduced by eastern whites and later western whites), into mutually suspicious groups that feared each other as possible agents of the invaders and slave hunters. This fear and suspicion, over a period of centuries, developed into dominating antagonisms like mutual hatred and dis-trust which made unity among the various groups a virtual impossibility. As the mutual fears and suspicions increased, the likelihood of any significant degree of unity decreased, and the degree to which Blacks suffered and were humiliated increased. What organized resistance to the invaders/enslavers that did exist was generally not enough, and as a result, foreigners came to dominate the entire continent.

But, as we noted, there is a historical basis which explains why unity among Blacks in Africa is so difficult to attain, even in the presence of such horrors as apartheid. For centuries, Our Brothers and Sisters there had to suspect everybody just to insure their survival!!! In order to merely stay alive, they had to distrust every face that was not familiar. But even under those pressures, they many times managed to seriously unite against their enemies. How could they, in an immediate and constant life and death situation, and without knowledge of who among them was the enemy, unite, while Blacks in America, who have no comparable fear of Blacks in general, fail to unite in any organized and meaningful way? Or, put in a manner that makes that question more relevant to Blacks in America, we ask, "Why don't We unite?" (Our Ancestors, faced with worse obstacles than We, were able to do so.)

In Part 1 of this essay, we stated that the keys to Black dis-unity were

Our acceptance of foreign ideologies (political integration and religious conversion) which fail to recognize Our color as a political factor. We pointed out that among the Black masses these type ideologies excite an instinctive repulsion which renders unifying with Blacks who take on a multinational stance impossible. That part of the essay did not fail to admit that there are other contributing factors to Our dis-unity, "but none that any sincere Black person would fail to dismiss in a time of crisis."

Since We are in a crisis situation, and lacking unity, We must conclude that insincerity is one of the contributing factors (particularly among Our community "leadership"). We will state it outright— there are very few Black persons/organizations struggling for the advancement of Our race (even though many claim to be). Since sincerity is a relative term, it must be defined according to the effort which is *needed* to bring about a projected end. What is needed to get Our race positively moving at this time are persons and organizations which are willing to give their all to Black People; persons and organizations which are prepared to give Our advancement priority over all other matters. We are not saying that all other matters should be disregarded or ignored. We are saying that Our advancement must get priority, and very few persons or community organizations are granting it that priority. Consequently (as a result), most of the things We attempt to do "to benefit the community" either fizzle out completely or fall short of their objective.

We will list a few examples of insincere participation. We are sure you have thought about these, and probably others.

(1) The tendency among Our community "leaders' to place personal and organizational goals and preferences above those which will most benefit Black People. Such organizations aim to support themselves at the expense of the Black Community. Their benefit to the Black community, if any, is actually incidental since their activities are planned primarily with the organization's welfare in mind.

(2) The tendency to thrive at the expense of the Black Community by rendering vital services to only a part of that community. (In other words, too many "community organizations" charge/overcharge Our community for

information, education and other necessities that are *vital* and must be made accessible to all of Us if we are to advance meaningfully. As such, those who do receive those services pay dearly money-wise, while those who need the services but can't afford to pay for them suffer moreso because they remain ignorant and needy. Ignorance and need are very expensive parasites.)

(3) The tendency to maintain a certain amount of *space* between you/your organization and certain parts (persons and sections) of the Black Community. (A community is a whole, Brothers and Sisters. If you claim to deal with the community, then you must be receptive to everybody in it. Additionally, a community organization must involve a high degree of community participation. Its membership should not work *for* the community nor at the expense of the community. It must work *with* the community for the advancement of the community, directing it if necessary.)

One factor that stands alongside insincerity and contributes to Our dis-unity is Our failure, as individuals, to take special measures which will control Our egos. (For the purpose of this essay, we will define an ego as an automatic self-serving response.) We are all aware that, during Our 400 years of captivity in this country, We have been the victims of overt and subtle processes which have made Us less and less Black and more and more non-Black. We resisted the affects of the overt processes, but the subtle processes crept into Us almost unnoticed. They virtually escaped Our attention as they carried out their mission of making Us act more and more like the people who enslaved Us and less and less like the People who civilized Us. Simultaneously (at the same time), Our Blackness, Our natural tendencies, ceased to exert themselves as automatic responses; they were replaced by the individualistic, ego-conscious responses which this environment encourages. Our failure to control these self-serving and self-protective responses handicap Us when We try to unite around a communal, self-sacrificing and self-critical structure.

Since Our Blackness is no longer an automatic response with Us, We must make **conscious** efforts to respond as Black People should respond (individually and organizationally). We must make **conscious** efforts to regain

Our inner being and, in so doing, eliminate the egotistic/foreign responses which force Us to insist that certain things must be done in certain ways in order to accommodate certain organizations or persons. We have to stop defending certain personal/organizational practices simply because we have ties with that organization. Also, We have to start accepting the fact that, when all of Us come together, "my" idea or "your" idea is not going to be implemented (effected/acted on), not because other ideas are necessarily better, but simply because we can only move in one direction at a time or implement one solution at a time. Work on more than one solution divides Us, and **We cannot afford to be divided.** A set of circumstances can demand that We act in a certain way; it cannot demand that We think a certain way. (In other words, Brothers and sisters, your actions will not always be a spitting image of your ideology.) All of Us have to realize this. If we don't, dis-unity will continue to plague Us.

A summary of this essay should reveal insincerity, Our failure to make conscious efforts to exert Our Blackness and control Our non-Black responses, and Our acceptance of foreign ideologies which deny Our uniqueness as the reasons for Our dis-unity. We will mention a pitiful additional reason— the general alienation of community "leaders" from the people they seek to unify. This will be approached in a later essay.

We ask all of you to remember that this is a life and death situation, not because Black People make it so, but because other people will have it no other way. They (other people) are not playing. They are not taking a casual approach to Our aspirations nor Our potential. Neither should We.

PEACE be with you, Brothers and Sisters, if you are willing to do what is necessary to get it.

31. "A Review"

In order to keep on top of things (stay alert), We should occasionally (from time to time) review what We learned from past experiences. Some of the lessons *The People* has learned are expressed in the following quotations:

"Time is the factor which separates the revolutionaries from the reactionaries. Time reveals who is serious about Nationhood and who is not. Time exposes those of Us who are "for real" about Our Blackness and segregates those who rant and rave and use Blackness as a platform aimed at relieving their individual frustrations and anxieties. Time, Brothers and Sisters, Time. Time will tell.

"Vision is necessary if We are to stand the test of time. Vision enables Us to peek into the future, to see where We are going, and to prepare for the obstacles which are going to temporarily hold Us back. If We can't see these things (obstacles and victories) beforehand, We will become disenchanted and use any setback as proof of the hopelessness of Our efforts, thereby excusing Ourselves from any further involvement.

"You can't see into the future with your eyes, Brothers and Sisters. You have to use your mind. But your mind must first be developed. Anyone can see from one day to the next, or from one week to the next; but this short vision won't prepare you to deal with a struggle which spans generations. To do this you have to understand, to the core, what has happened and what is happening."

"Until institutions are established which encourage mass revolutionary development, it is up to each of Us to discipline himself/herself and steer himself/herself toward a revolutionary frame of mind. All of Us can't wait for someone else to guide Us along. When one of Us has spare time, instead of taking a drink, listening to the radio or looking for some fun, that person should make himself/herself aware of Our history (all 7000 recorded years), the history of other peoples, and of fundamental laws which should be applied universally. The universal laws are particularly important because they prepare Us to deal with right and wrong as absolute values— as rules which do not change because of what a person has to gain or lose materially."

"One of the historical and present tragedies of Black individuals and organizations has been their tendency to consciously and/or subconsciously act in a manner that is contrary to what they seem to teach... We have to be certain that We don't use enemies of the community when We try to help the community. [For example,] if an organization has decided that capitalism is bad for the community, it should get a core understanding of capitalism which will enable its members to recognize capitalism however it appears. If an organization has decided that class consciousness is bad, organization members must be able to recognize that in all its forms. If an organization has decided that exploitation in general is the community's problem, that organization must be able to recognize exploitation in all its forms and degrees. Being able to recognize these negative forces will help Us avoid use of them when We attempt to do some good. Failure to avoid them could prove catastrophic in the long run."

"Why is it going to be so difficult to instill pride in Black People in the future, say 300 years from now? Because future Blacks are not going to know who their leaders were today. And why won't they know? Because nearly all of Us have Christian or Arabic names attached to Our Black bodies. A Black child 300 years from now will say, 'White people have names like Martin Luther King, Jr.,' and therefore think that King was probably white. Another Black child will say Malcolm X was an Arab because Black People don't have names like El Hagg Malik El Shabazz. Can you imagine that? Three hundred years from now Malcolm X might be identified as an Arab instead of a Black man simply because he innocently embraced a religion to replace the one that had been robbed from him...

"Of all the peoples on the face of the earth, none are more naturally spiritual and religious than Black People. Religion is that force which drives all of Nature's parts toward spiritual and physical harmony. Its purpose is to make Us freer and more loving, and in traditional Afrika it was represented by one Supreme God. It determined how Blacks acted toward one another on social, economic and political levels. Islam and Christianity, on the other hand, are religious ideologies which represent cultures that are dominated by economics and politics. Everything, including religion, revolves around efforts to make money, get land, and dominate others. Though they preach love and freedom, they practice deceit and enslavement; and history and their (the religions') emphasis on how converts identify themselves are proof of this."

"We should be constantly mindful of the historical fact that it is much more difficult to maintain a function that benefits the masses and depends upon the masses for continued success than it is to maintain a function that will benefit a select few. This is true because masses (large numbers) have a slower adjustment rate than small numbers. If an institution that benefits the masses shakes, the masses suffer tremendously; if an institution which benefits a select few shakes, that group can make a quick adjustment which might reduce the impact of the malfunction. This does not mean, however, that it is better to let institutions benefit a select few. Quite to the contrary, it is the reason why the masses should be completely involved in the institution-making process. Such involvement brings understanding, and understanding increases the ability of the masses to adjust quickly to malfunctions."

"We must be careful, We must be very careful, if We want the masses (all of Us) to progress. And We must be just as sincere. Which means, We have to work with the masses— not to get the masses to follow Us— but to inspire the masses to become self-determining and self-propelling. We must seek mass participation, mass understanding, and mass leadership. If any revolutionary thinks these are impossible aims, then he might as well hang up his revolutionary rhetoric. History has repeatedly...demonstrated that nothing less will do."

Instead of seeking integration, We should be seeking equality. "Equality is the right to control those institutions which affect Our lives and determine Our future. It is the right to determine how Our schools are run and what is taught in them. It is the right to establish a social and economic structure which fits Our views concerning production, distribution and general welfare. It is the right to be self-determining; the right to decide if We should pay taxes and, if so, how they should be spent. It is the right to establish a system of relationships which will be beneficial to Us, Black People. Equality has nothing to do with keeping up with whitey, individually or collectively. It has everything to do with Our natural rights, from the right to withdraw because of individual preferences, to the right to join Our forces, claim land which is due Us, and establish a government which will justly represent Our cause at the conference table of nations. That is equality, Brothers and Sisters. Nothing less will do!"

PEACE be with you, Brothers and Sisters, if you are willing to do what is necessary to get it.

32. "Alienation Among Blacks In America"

We will mention a pitiful additional reason (for Black dis-unity)— the general alienation of community leaders from the people they seek to unify (the community).   "The People Speaks" Vol. II, Essay 9

Within the Black Community in this country, there have developed two distinct groups; the one composed (made up) of those who are "aware" and who seem to be seeking, individually or collectively, an alternative to the established or dominant system, and the other composed of those who are not "aware" and who seem hopelessly entangled by the status quo/present system (because they have no practical nor common understanding of how to establish alternative institutions). The one we will refer to as "the intellectual vanguard," the other we will simply call "the masses."

We should stop and think for a moment... In which group do you belong?

What will be discussed in this essay is alienation. Since many of the readers of this essay might not know what alienation is, we will define it.

Alienation is a term which refers to the failure or inability of one group to *practically* identify with or interact with (that is, act in the interest of) another group.

Of great importance in that definition is the term "practical." We will define practical as "that which can be, or already is practiced or put into effect."

Let us go on. We have introduced the "intellectual vanguard" and the "masses", and we have defined the term "alienation." We will now tie the three together.

The process of becoming "aware" in this country, the process of understanding how a system functions, is also a process of taking on attitudes which will benefit the dominant system to some degree, even though you might be bitterly opposed to it, if you allow the system to manipulate you in any way, but particularly if you allow it to convince you that some elements or methods of procedure are indispensable (cannot be eliminated/must be used). The process of manipulation is intended to convert the seeker of knowledge into someone who supports the system, or into someone who is incapable of effectively opposing or attacking the system (in short, into someone who is incapable of establishing institutions which reveal the weaknesses and contradictions of the system's institutions). The process of manipulation is aided by the tendency of human beings to seek comfort or consolation out of life. The immediate outcome of this is that those who become "aware" somehow manage to remove themselves from the sickening environment which the "unaware" feel hopelessly and forever entangled in.

With that in mind we are able to characterize the "aware" person in the Black Community. That person believes that certain elements and methods must be used if anyone (or any group) hopes to establish institutions which will benefit Black People; and he/she (the aware person) does not relate to the day-to-day experiences of repression in the manner the masses do because the "aware" person has an outlet— he or she has something or somewhere to run to for relief. (We would not be too far off if we asserted that all "aware persons" assume at least one if not both of these characteristics.) Meanwhile, however, the masses have experienced no changes; they have known no relief.

(Perhaps it would be proper if we explained that the new environment or outlet of the "aware" person need not involve a physical change— that is, a change of location. Many times that is the case. However, it might, as well, be a mental change, a spiritual/emotional change, or a social change. The outlet might be represented by books or records (which have a "message"), religious involvement, or by an individual or group which might provide a sympathetic ear or an activity which will give the "aware" person's mind a few minutes of relief or "peace". The point is that the aware person has a positive/ meaningful escape valve. He/She is not confronted by "the system" all of the time.)

Again, we should stop and think for a moment. It is important that We recognize that, at this stage, two **mentalities** occupy the Black Community;

BLACK-SMART

the one which gets *some* relief and the one which gets *no* relief. Since we are dealing with the subject of alienation, we need not explore the mentality which gets no relief because it is not capable of alienating itself. It, without a moment's relief, feels hopelessly and forever entangled by the status quo/ present system. We will explore, instead, the mentality that gets some relief.

We have mentioned that that mentality, the "aware" mentality, has been manipulated by the system. How, and to what degree that mentality or person has been manipulated will become evident when he/she attempts to establish an alternative institution. (It will have its affect, as well, when an "aware" person isolates himself— that is, when he responds to his knowledge by doing nothing, by not attempting to establish any relationship with the community.) In this country the basis of the establishment's power is a politically disorganized mass which does not have a sound economic footing. An "aware" Black person would, therefore, see that the keys to Black Power are the political education of the Black masses and the establishment of a firm economic footing for Black People. The "aware" person would also recognize, in time, that capitalism will not benefit Blacks because it is anti-social and because the establishment's industrialists are too much in control of that economic activity. He/She, the "aware" person, would likely conclude that a socialist economy would most benefit Black People.

With those considerations, the "aware" persons have come up with a clear alternative to the status quo, an alternative which will benefit all Black People. Instead of capitalism, for example, they seek a socialist economy. Instead of an ignorant mass, they see the necessity of an educated mass. Why? Because they need a source of power, an element which can defy or negate the power of the establishment. That source of power is the active participation of the masses (as opposed to the general lack of participation of the masses which the present system encourages). The question is, "How do the 'aware' persons get the 'unaware' persons to respond to the program they introduce?"

In the Black community, those who are "unaware" want some basic changes, but they are unable to seek them, to initiate actions which would bring them about. If the "unaware" persons could see the "aware" persons' outline and understand them, or hear the "aware" persons' speeches and understand them, they would recognize that what the "aware" person has proposed might be a solution to their problems. However, the masses are not able to understand the "aware" persons' plans or speeches because the "aware" person refuses to speak in term and of processes that the masses can relate to. The masses are therefore reduced to having to watch what the "aware" persons do. What the "aware" persons do, in the absence of any initial support from the masses, is try to establish an economic footing which will support the alternative institutions which they have proposed. The "aware" persons almost always come to the conclusion that money is the key to that economic basis, and set out to get it. Unfortunately, the money belongs to the system. The "aware" persons recognize that one has to do certain things to get money in this system, and they set out to do them. In the process, they blow their final opportunity to get the support of the masses, who have to be convinced that something radically different is being attempted before they will participate. Instead of seeing a radical difference in the "aware" persons, they see a group which is about the business of making money. In the absence of any further understanding, the masses accept their activities as just another money-making venture, and refuse to respond in the manner desired by the "aware" persons.

The refusal of the masses to respond to the "aware" persons program insures the eventual failure of the "aware" persons efforts. The "aware" persons cannot effect substantial (real) changes without the support of the masses. An observer would have noticed earlier, with the appearance of the "two mentalities," that a basis for alienation has been established. That same observer would now notice that that basic difference has developed into a political liability for the entire community. That observer would notice that those persons who are potential leaders of the Black masses are unable to seek the necessary changes in a manner which will inspire the support of the masses; indeed, are unable to even communicate with the masses or adequately represent the yearnings of the masses. In short, the observer would notice that those who are "intellectually aware" (those potential leaders of the Black

Community) have established a barrier between themselves and their potential source of power (the masses).

For the third time, we should stop and think for a moment. We have just discovered that Black People in this country are almost totally dependent upon outside forces (both national and international) to bring about change that will substantially benefit the Black Community because those among Us who have the knowledge cannot effectively transfer that knowledge to the mass of people which has the power to force changes which will substantially benefit Us. Why are We in this shaky position? Because those who are "intellectually aware" insist on maintaining the barrier that only they can eliminate. As long as they remain in that state of consciousness, the Black Community in this country is going to be at the mercy of a whole lot of organized hostile political forces.

How do the "aware" maintain that barrier? Why hasn't it been eliminated? That question will be answered. First, though, we should mention that what has been written to this point suggests limitations to alienation among Us which in fact do not exist. We will tell you why.

What we have briefly sketched is one example of political alienation. We will go into more, but still inadequate, detail about political alienation and other forms of alienation as well, and hope you will realize how much of a curse it really is in Our community.

Political alienation is evident when a person or organization who has become aware of how an established system functions, and wants to establish or activate alternatives to that system, cannot adapt his/her responses to that knowledge to the reality which the masses of his/her people are confronted by daily. Political alienation is obviously found among established politicians who urge the community to follow an established systematic process which the community has no faith in. It is evident when persons consistently use terms and talk about processes which the masses do not understand, yet expect the masses to rally around them. It is demonstrated by the "aware" person who stays in his/her room and absorbs knowledge, yet fails to attempt to get involved in efforts to improve the community. Further, political alienation is demonstrated when local "leaders" who want to see some results (which they habitually confuse with substantial changes) attempt to struggle for the community instead of with the community. The outcome, in all instances, is Black inertia (nothing happens which really benefits the masses).

Closely allied to political alienation is cultural alienation. Culturally alienated persons usually relegate (or re-assign) politics to a secondary role and view cultural expression as the primary key to Black People progressing. Many of them probably adopted this attitude because they initially attempted to reach the masses with political propositions, noticed the lack of response from the masses, and gave up. What these persons seem unable to accept is the fact that cultural expression or acceptance is nurtured as a person or a people become aware of the role they have played and now play in the world order. It is an expressed appreciation of your race's influence and accomplishments. A people, like the Black masses, who have been taught that its race has contributed nothing to humanity is not equipped to give adequate support to a cultural program. Yet, as if this were not the case, the alienated person continues to push for the realization of Black cultural institutions. (This can be compared to trying to build a brick house without any bricks. You might end up with a house, but it won't be a brick house.)

Black People have "fun" (for lack of a better term) in many different ways, but there is no appreciation of anything political in that "fun." The occasions for fun engaged in by the Black masses can be used by the "intellectually aware" persons to get some political ideas across to them. But this is seldom done because "intellectually aware" persons are many times socially alienated. The "aware" person who is socially alienated refuses to view the social atmosphere of the masses as a practical arena for propaganda (the spreading of ideas). They refuse to accept the reality of the social life of the Black masses as an instrument of change. Social alienation, then, hinders the Black Community politically when such fertile arenas are left unexplored/uncultivated, and socially by maintaining the existence of several exclusive life-styles or social groups in Our community.

Finally, for the purpose of this essay, we will mention physical alienation. Some "aware" persons or groups don't want to deal with certain elements of the Black Community. They isolate themselves from those elements, or establish safeguards which insure no contact with those elements, and are therefore physically alienated. Physical alienation could be said to represent a complete withdrawal, since other forms of alienation likely preceded it (came before it). Simply put, physical alienation is the failure to stay in touch with the people we profess to care about. One of its immediate results is the inability of the "aware" person to seek changes which can satisfy the yearnings of the "unaware" persons (because the two do not have similar experiences/environments).

We have repeatedly used the term "substantial" when talking about changes which will benefit Black People. Substantial changes are changes which cannot be taken away without the occurrence of a serious confrontation. That implies that substantial changes are based upon forces or powers that you control, as opposed to being based upon a force that you do not control. For that reason, in order to make substantial gains it is important that We, Black People, develop a power base whose core or main strength lies in the Black Community. This cannot happen as long as the potential leaders of Our People alienate themselves from the masses and maintain that alienation.

Which returns Us to Our earlier question— "Why hasn't the barrier of alienation been eliminated?" Assuming that many persons do consider themselves serious seekers of change, we suggest that the following assertions largely answer the question.

(1) Those of Us who are "intellectually aware" are either extremely lazy mentally or we lack the creative intelligence which must be present in the leadership cadre of an economically oppressed group which is struggling for self-determination and liberation (if that struggle is to be successful). For one of these reasons (we suggest it is due to laziness rather than a deficiency), the leaders resort to practices which the system encourages. For example, we conclude that money is the key to economic survival instead of recognizing that, in the absence of land, Black People are that key. All leaders should be thinking of ways to make that potential economic force a productive economic force. Because of this reason also, we fail to struggle against the limitations

of language which confront Black People by failing to take those limitations into account when we attempt to communicate with the masses. The limitations of language and mental exploitation (miseducation), once overcome, will greatly reduce the number of non-participants. It is the job of those who are aware to figure out ways to overcome those limitations.

(2) Those of Us who are "intellectually aware" are either lazy physically or we lack the discipline which must be present in the leadership cadre of an economically oppressed group which is struggling for self-determination and liberation (if that struggle is to be successful). We suggest that persons among Us have a tendency to be lazy only at certain times; therefore we conclude that a lack of discipline explains Our deficiency here. This lack of discipline can help explain why Black "leaders" are so event-oriented. We are prepared to expend energy/work for short periods of time (from 4 to 8 weeks, once or twice a year), but are not prepared to do so for an extended period of time. This is unfortunate for at least two reasons:

a. an institution cannot be built, nor can a substantial change be brought about, by persons (the masses) who only witness or see Black alternatives to the status quo "at times", and

b. the system does not attack the masses or any Black person in spurts. It attacks Us all of the time. Therefore, We should be counter-attacking and fighting back all of the time. Leaders should be constantly preparing the masses for and exposing the masses to Black alternatives.

(3) Black "leaders" (the "intellectually aware") are trying to make strides in a political world at a time when they seem to have only a fingertips grasp of politics as a mechanism of control and change in the world. Because of this they make no attempts to solidify their power base by revolving that base strictly around factors which will be defended to the end by the Black masses, factors which are not likely to cause division among Black People. Instead, "leaders" get mixed up in fairy tale ideologies like the "third world", integration and unity with Muslims or Christians, etc. In short, they fail to realize that in order to get recognition in a political world, the heart of Our ideology will have to be Us as Black People with a Black perspective. What

"leaders" fail to realize, they can't strive for.

Politics is a power game (it should not be confused with "government"). If you are confused about the source of your power or if you try to cater to more than one potential power base at a time, you will certainly get wasted. Those of Us who call themselves "aware" had better accept that fact and reverse their wonderland theories before it is too late. We had better tie Our destiny, unequivocally (all the way), to that of the Black masses.

Right in line with the failure of Black "leaders" to realize how important a power base is in world politics is their failure to function with Black People in a politically healthy manner. In other words, if you preach an alternative it would be to your advantage if you practiced that alternative (even when times are hard). At all times, you and the organization you represent should be a functioning model of the ideas you preach to the masses about. If you preach to the masses about the evils of capitalism and then sponsor a dinner sale or a book sale to get needed funds, then the masses are going to resort to their usual activities when they need funds. We cannot build alternative institutions as long as We act in a manner that will insure the survival of existing institutions.

Alienation is a serious problem in the Black Community. Even if the masses somehow united themselves or rallied around an issue, it would be difficult for them to build institutions because those of Us who are prepared to build (those who have the required knowledge) would not be able to transfer that knowledge to the masses. This is pitiful indeed. It opens the door to Black genocide— the extermination of Us. Extermination is not a pleasant thing to be faced with.

We therefore leave all of the "aware" persons with a serious message. Any person or organization that alienates itself from the Black Community and is unable to reverse that process of alienation is not capable of leading that community to neither national consciousness nor self-determination. It is not capable of leading Black People to any substantial gains. After reading this essay, you can determine if you are alienated or not (you probably are). Then you can determine what you should do to help eliminate it.

PEACE be with you, Brothers and Sisters, if you are willing to do what is necessary to get it.

33. "Some Short Passages"

This essay will consist of several short passages which are related to Our/ Black development. Many of these will be dealt with in depth in later essays.

(1) Each of Us must always be honest with himself/herself. If you can't be honest with yourself, you can't function in a healthy manner with other members of the Black race. Each of Us must check out his/her mind and really discover and admit where he/she is coming from and why. Remember: A person who lies to himself is bad off, but a person who lies to himself and accepts the lie is bankrupt and incapable of straight thinking; a threat not only to himself but to Black People in general.

(2) Each of Us has to maintain at least two attitudes in order to make self-determination and communalism a reality for Black People. Each of Us has to maintain a humane, respectful, concerned, understanding and unselfish attitude toward Our People, and a political attitude toward those who do not sympathize with Our aspirations. What is a political attitude? For the purpose of this paragraph, a political attitude is a frame of mind that puts all sentimental feelings toward those who do not sympathize with Our just aspirations in a proper perspective. It is an attitude that defends what We have already established (as well as what We hope to establish), but does not exclude criticism because criticism is necessary for healthy development. It is an attitude of survival; an attitude which will allow Us to function on equal terms in this world without giving up those qualities which make Us Us. It requires a lot of conscious responses on Our part, and is therefore a large order, but an order which each of Us must fill.

While maintaining this political attitude We must not forget that there are oppressed people all over the world who cannot be ignored nor disregarded; people who must receive their just due. It is the duty of all of these oppressed groups to help each other. However, We must remember that Our concern must be concentrated among Ourselves at this point because racial solidarity will guarantee Our survival as a distinct people. Nothing else can give Us that guarantee.

(3) Many of Us have confused "intelligence" with "knowledge". Intelligence is a natural quality. It is there when each person is born. It has only to be nurtured, and this is done by exercising the mind (thinking-observing-listening-discussing-thinking). Knowledge, on the other hand, is being aware of "this thing" or "that thing." The harmful thing about knowledge is its exclusiveness (only a few persons really possess knowledge). This exclusiveness makes the absence of knowledge a liability, a great disadvantage. One term which generally describes such an absence of knowledge is "ignorance." The importance thing about ignorance is this: it causes a lot of intelligent persons to come to conclusions that are sometimes incorrect and sometimes unintelligent.

This brings Us to a realization which must be dealt with very delicately. That realization is that many Black persons who are very intelligent are also extremely ignorant. Their extreme intelligence does not benefit them or Black People because forces which are presently dominating Us do not reward intelligence, but their extreme ignorance harms them and the Black race because forces which are presently dominating Us do take advantage of what We do not know; they use what We do not know against Us. As a result, many of Us get involved in Our struggle and emphasize non-Black solutions to Our problems. Two cases will show this clearly:

a. There are intelligent Black persons who urge Us to unite with "workers of the world" against capitalism/imperialism. Such Black persons have come to the incorrect conclusion that things have changed; that "workers of the world" are supporting Us in larger numbers than ever before. What they fail to realize is that, in proportion to overall numbers, no noticeable change has taken place. The percentage of the "workers of the world" who support Us today is no larger than it was 100 years ago. In addition to not realizing this, many intelligent Black persons overlook other important factors. They seem to be ignorant of how "workers of the world" dealt with Black People hundreds of years ago and how they deal with Black People now (there is no difference). They seem to be ignorant of what "workers of the world" thought about Black People hundreds of years ago and how they think about Black People now (attitudes have not changed). Such Black persons also seem ignorant of what "workers of the world" sought (economically and socially) hundreds of years ago and what they seek now (the same thing, comfort at Our expense). If such Black persons had knowledge of these things they could not come to the unintelligent conclusions they come to.

[Note: An incorrect conclusion is one which should not be reached based upon the information available. An unintelligent conclusion is one which seems correct in theory but has been denied any practicality by historical circumstances and developments.]

(b) There are some intelligent Black persons who would have Us believe that the key to Our salvation is a foreign religious ideology and order. Such persons must be ignorant of the fact that religion is a force which will either dominate or be dominated/manipulated. Among white people, east and west, religion has not been a dominant, self-sustaining nor self-motivating force for nearly eight centuries. Instead, it has been used by people with a superiority complex to colonize and take advantage of "inferior" people. This took place when Christians went in search of riches and when Muslims went in search of land to live on, and it is still happening today.

A religion, at best, is an interpretation of life based upon people's responses to certain natural challenges to their survival. At worst, a religion is a political weapon which has a sleeping pill effect on its victims (those who had no part in its development). It follows then that neither of the better known religious ideologies of today will serve Our purpose. What an Arab develops to satisfy his uncertainties about his environment (and its happenings) will not satisfy the uncertainties felt by a man in Africa or Asia. As for Us adapting a religion which is intended to further the political aims of another group, even the thought is sickening. Those who do such a thing deserve a shameful fate, not only as a reward for being stupid but as a punishment for denying their Blackness and deserting their race.

No ignorance implies no religion that tells you that your color is not important. No ignorance implies a religion that recognizes you as an integral yet distinct part of Nature; a part that is no better or worse than any other part, but a part which definitely deserves to survive in its essence (its BLACKNESS).

(4) Each of Us has to play an **active** role; knowing what needs to be done is not enough. He who understands but has not committed himself to a definite plan of action is more of an obstacle than he who does not understand.

PEACE be with you, Brothers and Sisters, if you are willing to do what is necessary to get it.

What is *The People's Newsletter* all about? It is about a number of things, but they all revolve around the betterment of Black People in all parts of the world, but particularly here in America (since *The People's Newsletter* does not get to all parts of the world). We will mention a few of those things as they occur to us.

(1) We publish *The People's Newsletter* in order to get as many Black People as possible to think and talk about the same things at the same time. This recognizes that the most important key to Us getting power is not Our ideology or method, but Our unity. In other words, whether or not We do it together is more important than what We do or how We do it.

That is why we want Black People to be thinking and talking about the same things at the same time. It makes whatever is being discussed a popular issue, and people are more likely to support an issue and participate in its settlement if they feel that others are likely to do the same. In short, when a person feels that others are in the same frame of mind as he/she is, that person is not likely to worry too much about being left alone to suffer if he/she should take an active stand. He/She will feel certain that once a move is made, others will join in and take a stand as well.

(2) *The People's Newsletter* is meant to be a written review of issues facing Black People that can be read by the majority of Black People. We will add that reading is more than recognizing terms; it is understanding what those terms mean as parts of sentences and paragraphs. Our problem then, from the beginning, is twofold. We are writing to persons who do not recognize certain terms, and we are writing to persons who recognize many terms but fail to understand those terms as parts of a given sentence or paragraph. Additionally, we are writing to persons who fail to understand certain concepts (ideas) even if they are written in the simplest terms, terms which almost all of Us can recognize and define. Needless to say, as an instrument which most of Our

People can relate to, *The People's Newsletter* has been a huge failure.

But we are not going to let our past failures keep us from trying to succeed in the future. We are going to make *The People's Newsletter* as understandable to as many of Our people as we possibly can, but too many will be left out for as long as Black People fail to understand the English language. It should therefore be a priority of all of Our so-called community organizations to teach Our people how to read and understand English first, then teach them other languages. This is not to say other languages are not important, but faces the fact that understanding English is necessary for Our proper political development since all of Us in this country have to use that language each and every day, are influenced by the manipulation of that language each and every day, and are exploited by people who use that language to downplay and debase Us, even when We are present, each and every day. Not only should community organizations take the initiative in this area (We cannot rely on the public schools to do so— they are not meant to benefit Us), but each individual who recognizes that he/she is deficient in that regard should seek assistance, should seek to eliminate that deficiency/ weakness. Don't be ashamed to let someone know you can't read. Let them know that you are intelligent enough to realize that reading/understanding English is essential to Black People in this country. If We are unable to do so, the effectiveness of anything that is written by and for Black People in this part of the world will be hindered.

(3) We publish *The People's Newsletter* in order to make Black People aware of an ideology which We can rally around, which can be used as a basis for self-determination and nationhood, and which will help Us avoid the evils, like capitalism and racism, which generally victimize a large portion of most populations in the world. This ideology has been called Communalism, African Socialism and other things, but its essence is aware Black People who are active, it revolves around aware Black People who are active and it must be institutionalized by aware Black People who are active. We must know that there are alternatives/choices to this system that certain people are now operating/controlling, We must know that Black People alone can initiate/start

either of those alternatives and make it a success, and We must realize that if We do not institutionalize an alternative, it is because of Our shortcomings, Our failures, and not because of what some other group of people did to slow Us down.

We call for an ideology which involves the masses, which seeks the support of the masses, which looks to the masses for success or failure. Since, then, the masses are the key, the masses must be the active and aware Black People we spoke of in the earlier paragraph. Therefore, a Black ideology must revolve around the educating, mental development and politicizing of the masses of Our People.

(4) We publish *The People's Newsletter* in order to reveal many of the contradictions among Black People that keep Us from moving, that keep Us from making real progress. More directly put, we publish *The People's Newsletter* in order to tell you, the reader, and other Black persons what you do that indicates and proves that you are not ready to be free, are not ready to determine your own destiny, are not ready to build a nation that will represent the will of Black People; and we dare you to challenge such a statement by simply asking you to check yourself out. You ask why certain things keep oppressing you and why certain changes don't come about; we say because you don't act to bring them about.

[You don't support the things which are designed to benefit you, but you are quick to say that "niggers ain't ready to do nothing." Why do you have to wait for the "niggers" Brothers and Sisters? Aren't you ready to do anything?

Sure you're ready to do something. You're ready to get a college degree and make something out of yourself. That's exactly what you're going to do, you are going to make yourself a chump. Don't you realize, after all this time, that this system is not designed to help you "make it," regardless of whether you have a degree or not. But you want to buy a house and some land so your children won't have to struggle like you did; so they'll have a start in life. That's a noble idea, but have you stopped to wonder about the chances of your children keeping that house and land? Unemployment is getting worse, the cost of living is steadily increasing (going up, up, up)— where are your children going to get the spare money to keep up the house payments? Those white people's uncle is going to force them to sell it, or take it and auction it off to the highest bidder. That will make your noble effort extremely silly indeed.

Or maybe you have decided to invest your money in this white man's future by buying stocks and bonds and enabling those racists in South Africa and America to kill people who look just like you look. Or maybe it would be better to put your money in a savings account? The dollar is worth 60 cents (1977), and twenty years from now it will be worth a quarter. That doesn't sound like a very good pension, but crumbs and peanuts satisfy some people.

You become frustrated. You put on some dark glasses and a frown, throw your fist in the air, talk trash about whitey and yell "Revolution, Revolution," but you insist on doing things your way. You can't work with anyone else because your problem is a personal problem, and you're looking for a solution that is personally rewarding. You want people to follow *you*, but when the people fail to rally around your screams (which don't define a plan), you withdraw into your own world. You take an individual approach to a social problem. You ask questions hoping to get an answer which will justify your personal/individual approach. You don't have time to work with a community organization because you have to provide for your wife and child, for example. When you feel it's time to relieve the mental and emotional pressures and "expand your mind," you don't do community work or try to get some knowledge, you reach for a jay. It's time to get high or drunk or stoned. Go ahead— Malcolm X got high before he got serious about liberating Black People. And you'll do the same; you'll get high before you get serious about liberating yourself and other Black People.

You don't like what's going on in this country, but all you can think about right now is a party. There's nothing wrong with a party— if you have something to party about. Take the Rockefellers, for example. They have something to party about; they are on top of the world. They and the Kennedys and DuPonts party all week long because they have some happy and passive Negroes on their hands. They hit Negroes upside the head with blackjacks, they shoot Negroes in the back, they play ignorant Negro males against ignorant Negro females, they watch Us scramble for unemployment compensation and welfare, and they call Our women when they want to be sexually satisfied. And Our women go to them, and the Rockefellers party all night long with them, so naturally you should party all night long too, Bro.

You're cruising along in that Coupe de Ville or Triumph, and you're looking cooler than death. Everybody can see who is behind the steering wheel, but nobody can quite figure out if you are driving the car or if the car is driving you. But you don't care (neither does the car) because you don't have anywhere to go anyway. You're just waiting for the revolution to start, right?

Looking at tv all night long is like donating your mind to CBS. You just love to listen to that "blue eyed soul" sing down to you. Did you just ask your Brother what's happening? Did you ask him because you don't know?

You can't afford to give $5.00 a month to a community organization, but $25.00 a month at concerts, clubs and McDonald's don't cause a strain.

You sure do know a lot Brother. You can tell anybody all about Our struggle. By the way, which organization did you say you were working with? What did you say you had done to help Us move forward? You say you keep up with what's happening by reading certain newsletters? That's good, Blood, but how do you participate? What do you do??

Somebody said, "a nigger ain't shit", but that ain't true. You can't convince us that you ain't shit Brother, and neither can you Sister, no matter how hard you try.]

(5) We publish *The People's Newsletter* in order to inform Black People of what America and other racist governments are doing, to reveal the contradictions of the present systems, and explain how those racist actions and contradictions can be used to railroad Black People. We try to get you to think about what is going on in the world and relate what is going on to your personal experiences. If white people don't like Black People in Zimbabwe

(Rhodesia), they don't like Black People in the United States of America. If a religion has not benefited the mass of the people who created it, how do you figure it is going to benefit the mass of Black People? Congress just said it is going to take a minimum of $2.85 (1977) an hour to live? Why then is Congress going to take 30% of that $2.85 for taxes, etc. The government pays farmers not to plant while Black People starve to death. White people can't reproduce in large numbers, so they attempt to control Our/Black births with pills, abortions, planned parenthood and similac. England has a new political party which plans to remove all Black People from that country within the next 20 years. Will whites in America come up with a similar solution to their race problem? Does it matter?

The 80 million Black People in Brazil can't even talk about race and their wretched condition; it's against the law. The law is in America too. Michael Manley is trying to help Black People in Jamaica, and the United States is trying to kill him dead; just like they killed Lumumba in the Congo, Biko in South Africa, and Fred Hampton here. Just like they'll try to kill anybody who tries to help someone who looks just like you look.

Everything that happens is related to you, Sister, and you, Brother. *The People's Newsletter* tries to get you to think about what is happening and figure out what the relation is. As a matter of fact, you should stop and think after you read each article in order to make sure you get the message that each article carries.

For basic information concerning the purpose of *The People's Newsletter*, we suggest you review Essay 6 of The People Speaks.

PEACE be with you, Brothers and Sisters, if you are willing to do what is necessary to get it.

35. "Toward An Understanding Of Africa"

The major problem confronting Africa today is outside interference; outsiders force themselves on the African People and certain Africans aid outsiders by going to them for assistance. This is not only true today, but has been so for thousands of years. A brief flashback on history will reveal this trend.

Africa, all Africa, is the native homeland of Black People. Long before any non-Blacks entered upon the scene, Black People had developed the greatest civilization known to man. They had developed writing, the sciences, engineering, medicine, architecture, religion and the fine arts to very refined degrees. This civilization was taken to what is now called Egypt by Black People, and it was in Egypt, **before the intrusion of any non-Black person,** that African civilization reached its highest heights, heights which to this day have not been equalled. In time this advanced civilization was lost/destroyed, and many factors were involved; but one which promoted the disintegration was the appearance of non-Blacks who wanted to turn the Land of the Blacks into the land of the Arabs.

The great advancements which the African People had made, the grand states and empires they had established, were viewed as roadblocks to Asian/ Arab objectives in Africa. They attempted to eliminate these empires, and the elimination attempts were stepped up by Muslim onslaughts after the rise of Islam in the 7th century A.D. Later, when European whites saw that Africa was a land filled with mineral wealth (gold, diamonds, etc.), they began to challenge the Asian whites for control, while at the same time joining the Asians in asserting that Africans had no history worthy of note. They debased the African culture and initiated economic restraints against persons who insisted on holding onto their African-ness, with the end result of forcing many Africans into classifying themselves as Arab/Muslim or Christian (it helped them to "get over"). Both groups, eastern and western whites, worked hard in the past and still do so today to keep Us from realizing that We need not be dominated by them.

Both white groups want to dominate the world, and they view Black People as pawns that can be abused, exploited and manipulated in whatever way necessary to bring about their aims. If Blacks think at all, whites want Us to think in terms of white objectives; they don't want Us to think that We should have objectives of Our own. In case some of Us do think in terms of Black/ Africa, whites try to prove them incapable.

White people initiate measures meant to hinder Black nations. For example, Arabs who scream about Black brotherhood charge Black nations, which are poor to start with, unusually high prices for oil (thereby hindering the economic development of that nation) and use their position in the OAU (Organization of African Unity) to hinder the political development of Africa as a Black-dominated continent. In that same stream, British/Americans try to give the impression that they are the keys to a settlement of hostilities in Southern Africa, instead of admitting that the Blacks there will eliminate the problem quickly if the outsiders would leave. Additionally, the Russians are supplying arms to both Ethiopia and Somalia, keeping them able to fight each other, while the Arabs use Islam first to get Eritrea to declare itself independent from Ethiopia and then to get Somalia to declare war on Ethiopia, thereby hoping to remove Ethiopia as a political obstacle to the spread of Islam/Arabization and making the rich Eritrean province part of the economic base of the Arabic world. There are many more cases which can be mentioned just as easily.

Whites constantly claim that the great civilization which flourished in Egypt thousands of years ago can be traced to white origins. In fact, the only noticeable thing about Egypt or any other part of Africa that can be traced to white origins is the turmoil that constantly afflicts the continent. Arabs and Americans, Jews and Europeans, etc. refuse to allow the African People to conduct their own affairs. They insist on telling Black People what to do, or use their enormous military and economic powers, together with some unthinking toms, to cause chaos when the African People resist their insanity. Thus, whites continue to rule Southern Africa, confusion reigns in Angola and

Zaire, Ethiopia is in shambles, Kenya bows to Israel, and Islam turns Africans (at home and abroad) into third and fourth class Arabs. To eliminate this confusion and to eliminate the confusion that afflicts the minds of Black People everywhere, the foreign element must be eliminated/expelled.

Begin to understand Africa, Brothers and Sisters in America, and you begin to understand yourself. Begin to understand what afflicts Africa, and you begin to understand why Black People over here can't seem to "get it together."

PEACE be with you, Brothers and Sisters, if you are willing to do what is necessary to get it.

BLACK-SMART

36. "The Nigger Factory"

America is a nigger factory, Brothers and Sisters. America can brag that it produces the best qualified niggers in the greatest numbers anywhere in the world. But the factory is not what we will be concerned about in this essay. We will talk instead about the niggers which are produced, and hope that this will be a step toward transforming them into Black People who will, in time, close the factory down.

Before we go further, we will define a few terms:

(1) *Nigger* A person who fails to do those things which will most benefit him/her. Neither education, financial status nor class, nor any other thing like that, can be considered a factor when trying to determine if a person is a nigger or not. The only factor that is to be considered is whether he/she does those things which will most benefit him/her.

(2) *Nigger Leader* A person who tries to convince a people (in this case Black People) that he/she will assume primary responsibility for bringing about changes that will benefit the masses of that people. Nigger leaders know they can't bring about any worthwhile changes, but they want the people to think they can and hope that such thoughts by the people will keep the people from "taking care of business" in a hurry. Nigger leaders don't want the people to take care of business (for various nigger reasons), so they try to control the people by convincing the people that they, "leaders", are going to do what is necessary and therefore deserve the allegiance of the people.

(3) *Nigger Group* Two or more niggers who get together periodically or work together regularly for an expressed or implied reason or purpose. Their purpose is limited in scope (it does not primarily concern itself with the whole, that is, all Black People), and many times it is aimed toward personal gratifications or conveniences. The niggers involved think so much of their group and its personal benefits that they have a hard time convincing themselves that their nigger group is expendable (can be done away with, should become part of another group).

BLACK-SMART   125

(4) *Nigger Factory*   Whatever produces niggers and nigger groups as a **matter of course.** Nigger factories are one of America's natural defense mechanisms. To eliminate a nigger factory is to seriously cripple whoever owns the factory. As stated earlier, nigger factories will not be dealt with in this essay.

NOTE: NO ONE should expect any person to admit that he/she is a nigger, a nigger leader, that he/she belongs to a nigger group or that he/she benefits from a nigger factory. However, all Black persons should be able to recognize niggers, nigger leaders, nigger groups and those who benefit from nigger factories. We need to be able to recognize them because niggers, nigger leaders and nigger groups hold Black People back by getting Us to waste time working/bull-jiving with them. We need to be able to recognize those who benefit from nigger factories because they will have to be "controlled" once We close the factories down.

[Additionally, the term "nigger" is a very relative term— it might take on a different meaning wherever you go, ranging from a very negative thing to a very close friend. Don't get hung up on the word; just keep the given definitions in mind. That way, all of Us should get a clear understanding of who is being discussed here.]

We will begin with niggers. Niggers come in all shapes and sizes; they are found on street corners, in downtown offices and "progressive" night clubs; they do anything from snatching purses from little old women to drawing paychecks from state and local governments. They are programmed to destroy themselves, to keep themselves and others like them from developing properly (as human beings should develop). Many of them are niggers because of personal weaknesses; they are so overpowered by the injustices that surround and afflict/victimize them that they feel helpless to do anything but cop out. They cop out by committing petty crimes, by acting uppity and by being "cool"; they ambush their bodies with heroin, coke and marijuana, wine and whiskey, pills and cigarettes, etc., and use all of their energies on cars and motorcycles, chasing the opposite sex, and generally ignoring the well-being of themselves and anybody else they come into contact with. Others are

BLACK-SMART

niggers not because of the aforementioned personal weaknesses, but because they would rather satisfy their own petty ambitions than work for the benefit of their race. These niggers "make it"; they get a house, two cars and the opportunity to act like white people. To them, integration is desirable because it requires less of their time and energy and keeps them from having to cast their lot with the majority of their race. Then there is a third collection of niggers. Such niggers are, pure and simple, so scared of the power of white people that they wouldn't even dare think about opposing whites by trying to improve the life of the masses of Black People. These are the super niggers, the ones who have to whisper when they mention a term like "racist" or "prejudiced". These niggers are afraid to sign a petition which is not government approved because they might lose their job or cause the FBI to start a file on them. All three of these nigger types specialize in wasting time (not doing anything productive). They either don't try to get an understanding of the factors that control their lives, or ignore that understanding if they happen to run across it. In short, we repeat, they don't take measures which could benefit them and their race. This is unfortunate.

Some niggers love nigger leaders (see definition). They love nigger leaders because nigger leaders are not a threat to the present system and will therefore not call for their nigger admirers to confront the power structure in any meaningful way. Actually, such an unwillingness to confront the power structure makes nigger leaders kind of unimportant insofar as domestic (inside America) concerns go. But, that's okay because they aren't worried about their lack of power/status. That is because nigger leaders pride themselves on unreal stuff like charisma (personal charm) and verbal militancy (threatening talk). White people recognize their charisma and weaknesses, and appoint them to "leadership" status by giving them scant national or local exposure and a few dollar bills. This satisfies the ego of the national leaders since it allows him or her to fantasize about being "somebody'. It is important to point out that nigger leaders do not become a factor with aware members of his/her race because the persons recognize them for what they really are. The aware persons realize that neither charisma nor talk will make Us a liberated People.

They also realize that anyone who gets national attention/exposure at a time when We don't control any media facilities is not to be trusted. A few years ago, maybe; but now, no way.

So it is easy to see that nigger leaders have no respect in the Black Community and are not likely to seriously organize Black People. This task must be attended to by persons who are aware and actively seeking an alternative/choice to the present system. We have characterized such persons in earlier essays, and must do so again, but first we must deal with a very important production of the nigger factory. That production is the nigger group.

Nigger groups are a trip. Still, they are important because they bring niggers together under a common banner. Unfortunately, it is a banner of do-nothingness (that is, do anything but what is necessary). Nigger groups call themselves automobile clubs, fraternal/brotherhood and religious orders, sewing clubs, and community organizations, among other things. We do not feel it is necessary to give our readers a rundown on each of these types. Most of them don't need to be analyzed to be understood (their objectives are that simple/shallow). However, because nigger groups which call themselves community organizations usually have some type of professed political base and are made up of niggers who are somewhat "aware", we feel it is necessary to expose them by revealing what they do that shortchanges the Black Community, the very community they claim to want to lead to self-determination and nationhood.

The professed aim of the community organization in the Black Community is the betterment of Black People, the masses of Black People (that is, the elevation of Black People to Our proper place on the scale of human dignity). One key to bringing this is educating Black People in a variety of areas. [Education is a key because it is a stepping stone to uniting Black People. Once We unite, We can bring about the type of social order which will benefit Us because its objectives will be the betterment of Black People.] We have to be educated in schools, in classrooms, at lectures and speeches, at rallies, etc. We have to be educated about Our history and the history of man in general; We have to be educated so We can read, write and do mathematics, and grasp an understanding of certain principles that govern human relationships, etc. These principles are usually called economics, government, international affairs— the social order. Young children need to be taught these things, as do older children, teen-agers, and adults. In short, each Black person must be educated in order to understand how the overall social order affects him/her, and how he/she, by acting in certain ways, can affect and drastically change the overall social order.

Community organizations realize the importance of education, for example, and take deliberate steps to bring about an educated mass. Community organizations also realize that the educational process transcends (goes beyond) deliberate or calculated efforts. They realize that, just as important as the classroom or lecture is the practice of the organization itself, so they concern themselves with doing those things which are consistent with the ideology expressed in their educational process. Thus, community organizations lay out a plan of attack/development, run into difficulties, discover new methods and approaches, discover previously unknown allies (Brothers and Sisters who are struggling), relate to and unite with these new allies (since the educational process has revealed that unity, above all else, is necessary if a people is to liberate itself), make readjustments to increase efficiency (some create new organizations by eliminating a number of old ones) and advance. Community organizations realize that they must act according to what the educational process has taught them if they expect the masses to realize the full value of the educational process which they, the masses, are encouraged to pursue/seek.

Nigger groups of a political nature, it seems, don't recognize a relationship between what they teach and what they do. Nigger groups might see education as a key to Black progress/development, and their educational process might stress unity and efficiency as political necessities, but they fail to act according to those dictates. A nigger group, for example, will start an educational program and become more concerned about the survival of their program than they are about what will most benefit the Black Community. They will see that it is difficult to get a school going because of monetary shortages and lack of teachers, etc. They begin to struggle and, while struggling, discover other groups which are involved in the same type educational efforts and faced with the same type problems. Yet they fail to eliminate many of the problems by refusing to combine the two efforts. All groups concerned prefer to make their effort ("thing") successful. They casually compete for necessities and rip the Black Community off in order to get needed funds. Efficiency is crippled and the Black Community suffers. Why? Because some nigger groups have failed to act according to the principles which they want to teach the Black masses.

It doesn't stop there. It is unfortunate, but nigger groups get many more opportunities to demonstrate their lack of concern for the Black Community. Nigger groups get many more opportunities to leave negative impressions on the masses of Black People, in short, to turn the masses off. For various reasons, nigger groups might need headquarters, might not be able to afford one, yet refuse to share one with a community organization or another nigger group. Additionally, nigger groups refuse to participate in efforts to project an image of a united Black Community. They refuse to become part of an umbrella organization, for various nigger reasons, yet continue to talk about the value of unity and concerted action. And, nigger groups refuse to permit such an umbrella organization to become "the" organization. They refuse to accept the fact that, even though hundreds of small organizations may exist in theory and actually carry our certain singular activities, in practice, if Black People are to benefit in substantial degrees, only one organization can get functional priority. This one organization must be able to command primary allegiance from all of the progressive elements in the community if that is necessary to adequately effect an ideal (build an institution). Nigger groups scorn such a thought. They argue that such an arrangement cannot work, and might point to an incident in history to "prove" their point. The fact of the matter is that nigger groups want their membership to promote the platform/ ideas which they sponsor first and foremost. Their "proof" of past failures partially obscures and camouflages their niggerness, and totally ignores one fact— persons, not the organizations they build, determine if that organization is successful or not successful.

On that note, we will bring this essay to a close. We hope our readers will be able to determine why certain things which need to be done in Our community are not done. We hope our readers will be able to understand why certain groups who say they are anti-"this" and pro-"that" practice "this" instead of "that". We hope our readers, by applying the information available, will be able to determine who the culprits are in the Black Community and what their game is. Don't allow yourself to get hung up on "good intentions"; such considerations have no place in a serious struggle. The essential fact, represented by what is done or not done, is all that matters.

A nigger is a nigger, Brothers and Sisters. They and all things related to them must be exposed/eliminated.

PEACE be with you, Brothers and Sisters, if you are willing to do what is necessary to get it.

37. "YOU"

YOU are power. The very person who is reading these lines represents a force which can bring about changes that few imagine possible at this time. Don't sell yourself short. Don't doubt yourself. YOU have the ability to observe what is going on around YOU. YOU have the ability to hear what people say and compare what they say with what they do. Based on that comparison, YOU can determine if they are serious about what they say, or if they are just trying to run a game on YOU.

YOU are intelligent enough to decide what needs to be done to make life worthwhile for the masses of Black People. As YOU become aware of additional factors, YOU will be able to use your intelligence to figure out how the thing that needs to be done can best be done. Your mind is just as powerful as the next person's mind. Don't let the next person convince YOU otherwise.

Since there are a lot of ways to do what needs to be done, and since a united effort is needed to make either of the ways/methods successful, it is important that the powerful minds which make up the Black Community organize. Organizing is necessary. Each person who has begun to use his/her mind is capable of organizing persons in the community who have not started to think in political terms. At the same time, the persons who are thinking should seek out others who are thinking so they can organize their different thoughts around a plan of action that will result in one mass movement instead of several small movements. The key to this is recognizing that only one plan can be dealt with effectively at a time. That means that many persons who have very good ideas about how certain things should be done must be willing to rally around a plan of attack that does not necessarily include what they thought of.

YOU will recognize the necessity of the organizing process. Don't let others convince you that you need to join them before you can get the process

BLACK-SMART

started, because YOU are just as capable of organizing as other persons. But in order to see the process become a success, YOU must join with others, teach others and learn from others; and YOU *will be able to do so.*

After YOU have organized others and organized with others around a plan of action that will result in one mass movement, certain moves will have to be made. YOU will have reached the point where acting/action takes on a primary role. The aim of these actions will be the building of institutions which serve to benefit the masses of Black People. The aim of these actions, in other words, will be the establishment of a force which can keep other forces from having a bad influence on YOU and your people. YOU can help build these forces/institutions; YOU can help establish a Black force that will keep other forces from taking advantage of US. Don't allow anyone to tell YOU otherwise.

YOU can do what anyone else does. YOU are as intelligent as anybody else is. YOU can observe, YOU can come to decisions, YOU can organize and YOU can act/build. That makes YOU just as powerful as the next person.

Remember Sister, Remember Brother; YOU are power. YOU can help do what needs to be done to elevate Black People. YOU can also fail to do what needs to be done; YOU can let other people slight YOU and run all over YOU (and other Black People in the process). To do or fail to do; therein lies your choice. Please choose intelligently.

PEACE be with you, Brothers and Sisters, if you are willing to do what is necessary to get it.

38. "Know Where You Stand"

The Jews didn't know where they stood in Germany in the 1930s, Brothers and Sisters. Too many of them allowed the Germans to mislead them. Too many of them accepted ideas and information they should have rejected, and rejected ideas and information they should have accepted. As a result of this, as a result of not knowing whose side they were really on, or where they really stood, six million of them got slaughtered.

Don't make the same mistake the Jews made, Brothers and Sisters. Don't be confused about whose side you are on; KNOW WHERE YOU STAND. This is important because knowing where you stand will determine how you interpret what you read and what goes on in this country and the world.

Know where you stand in relation to white people in this country. Understand that white people have had since 1619, almost 360 years, to grant Us the liberties which any human being has by right of birth. Understand that they have not granted Us Our rights in so long a time because they never intended to grant Us those rights and still don't intend to grant Us those rights. Understand that We will get what We deserve as human beings only when We take Our destiny, Our future, into Our own hands.

Know where you stand in relation to "liberals" in this country, particularly white liberals. Understand that white people have been helping Us get what they want Us to have ever since they helped drag Us off the slave ships, *but they have never been willing to help Us get what We wanted to get*. The white "socialists" and "communists" of today (just like the white revolutionaries of the 1920s and 1930s, and just like the white "liberals" of the 1960s and 1970s) want Us to move in a direction that will not threaten their definition of what the world order should be. They want Us, Black People, to get involved in their white family argument, but they don't want Us to introduce Our own solutions to the problems that afflict Us because We might seek to destroy the one thing all of the "socialists" and "communists" and "liberals" want to keep alive; We might seek to destroy white supremacy, and none of the white groups are progressive enough or revolutionary enough to seek the destruction of that.

Know where you stand Brother, and you too Sister, because that knowledge will determine whether you stand or fall. It will determine whether you ask or beg. It will determine whether you lead or follow, whether you walk or crawl, and whether you laugh or cry, etc. It might even determine how long you live, or how soon you die.

And know another thing, Black People. Understand that where you stand is not your decision alone to make. The Jews thought they stood with the Germans simply because they had decided to stand with the Germans. They soon discovered, too late, too late, that the Germans had other ideas. *The Jews discovered that it is not enough to pick the side you want to stand with. Even more important is that you pick the side that is willing to stand with you.*

Know where you stand, Brothers and Sisters. Even if you don't understand anything else, understand where you can go for certain protection when things start getting hot. If you don't understand that, you will probably end up in the middle of a cross-fire or in the torture chamber of the enemy.

Stand with your Brothers and Sisters. Stand with the people who look just like you look and experience just what you experience. Stand with Black People.

PEACE be with you, Brothers and Sisters, if you are willing to do what is necessary to get it.

39. "Are You Scared?"

Does violence scare you Brother, or you Sister? Since you have been victimized by it for such a long time it shouldn't, but if it still does you had better do something that will keep these racists from scaring you to death. What had you better do? You had better let the violent racist know that you can get violent too. You had better prepare yourself to defend yourself.

PEACE be with you, Brothers and Sisters, if you are willing to do what is necessary to get it.

BLACK-SMART

40. "To Be Black, Or Not To Be Black"

White people are opposed to the very *idea* of Us, Brothers and Sisters; not so much because Black People have weight and occupy space, but because Black People represent a spiritual and mental force which opposes their insanity. Black People should never fail to have this in mind. Black People are a threat to whites because they, whites, have made it so, if for no other reason. They cannot see Us being Ourselves without simultaneously (at the same time) feeling Us rejecting them and desiring to get them for what they have done to Us. Remember that. If they "like" you, then it is because you do what they want to see you do; if they don't "like" you, it is because they feel threatened by you; it is because you don't make a *special* effort to make them feel comfortable.

To be Black or not to be Black; that is the question that confronts each and every one of Us today. If We feel integration is necessary, if We feel We have something to prove to them, if We talk softly when one of them approaches, or if We feel We need them in order to advance, then We have chosen to not be Black. On the other hand, if We take the attitude that they have something to prove to Us, that they need to integrate with Us for their survival, that they need Us in order to progress, and We have no reason to fear what they hear Us say, for examples, then We have chosen to be Ourselves/Black. The choice is simple.

What We choose will express how We feel about their claims of superiority. If we play their game **because it is their game**, We at the same time admit that they are right when they claim that they are superior to Us. But, if We attempt to do things Our way, according to a set of values and principles that are Ours, then We at the same time challenge their claims of superiority.

How We act when dealing•with whitey, no matter how trivial/small the dealing might seem, will determine how whitey acts when he deals with you/

US. If We/you smile when there is nothing to smile about (because you think whitey wants you to smile), or fail to demand that which is rightfully Ours, then We have expressed a lack of racial pride and self-esteem. Whites realize this and treat Us accordingly. However, when We/you determine how We respond to whatever, regardless to who is around, and when We demand that which is rightfully Ours, then whitey treats Us with respect because he knows We/you will not tolerate any disrespect.

Do We demand respect by asserting Our right to be Black? Or do We prepare a grim future for Black babies by singing, dancing, praying, damning whitey and not laying the foundation for Black institutions? We have a proper view and perspective now, Brothers and Sisters, and We should know what pitfalls to avoid. Let Us be about the business of avoiding them. Let Us be about the business of Blackness.

PEACE be with you, Brothers and Sisters, if you are willing to do what is necessary to get it.

41. "Are Black People Serious?"

When a person complains about being oppressed, when a person complains about ill-treatment at the hands of someone else, when a person complains that his tax dollars are not being used to benefit him, and when a person complains that missiles are being built when hospitals are what's needed, for examples, that person has begun to take an interest in the forces that will determine the quality of his life and, to some extent, the duration/length of his life. When that same person says he wants to be free to decide what is best for him and his kind, and insists that he will lay his life on the line in order to get some freedom, then that person seems to be ready to take control of those forces that will determine the quality of his life and, to some extent, the duration/length of his life. But, when that same person who seems to be ready to take control of his destiny smokes a cigarette that he knows will give him cancer or make her bleed internally without warning, or injects a drug into his body that he knows might, for various reasons, lead to permanent injury or instant death, or smokes a jay that he knows will retard (slow down) his bodily processes and render him sexually impotent (unable to contribute to the conceiving of a child), or drinks a mixture that he knows will destroy his brain, his liver and his co-ordination, etc., then one has to wonder about this person. One has to wonder if he has seriously thought about the things he says; if he is indeed serious. One has to wonder if he is concerned about the quality of his life only when he is not in a position to control it. One has to wonder, Brothers and Sisters, if he is only concerned about himself in an abstract sense (Persons who deal only in the abstract aren't serious about applying their thoughts to everyday life).

This essay is not an attack on cigarette smokers, alcoholics (including "casual" users) or drug users/addicts who preach Black Power. It simply recognizes that the role these persons have to play in Our liberation is a crucial one, particularly from a standpoint of time.

It can be correctly said that you are oppressed because it is convenient for someone else to oppress you. You are ill-treated because it is convenient for someone else to mistreat you. Your tax dollars are not being used to benefit you because somebody else wants to use them for something else. And, hospitals are not being built because it is to somebody else's advantage (convenience) that missiles be built. However, convenience is no justification for what they do to you. That is why it is correct for you to take an interest and, if possible, take control of the forces which determine the quality of your life. The question is, "Are you ready to take control?"

It is true that, to some extent, you are already in control of your body. And, we are certain that you want to live with as few diseases and sicknesses as possible. Yet, you keep on smoking those cigarettes. You are destroying your lungs, but it doesn't matter because you would prefer to light up. You expose yourself to cancer, seizures and instant death, but you don't mind because it is convenient (you can have fun?) for you to take the pill, smoke jays and shoot shit. And you kill your brain cells and destroy your liver, but you don't mind because it is convenient for you to get "stoned". From one day to the next you mistreat your body, knowing all the time that you are going to need your body to liberate yourself from those people who take advantage of you. Really now, are you serious?

At no time have drug users, drug addicts or casual alcoholics been responsible for bringing about the type changes that must be brought about in the Black community. But many promising minds and leaders have wasted away and/or died early due to diseases and sicknesses that would not have occurred if those persons had not introduced so much filth into their bodies. Thousands of years of history make those points clearly, Brothers and Sisters, and We, Black People, are going to be the next example history can point to to prove this assertion if We don't make the necessary adjustments.

Brother, Sister, something is slowing Black People down, holding Us back, keeping Us from moving forward at the speed We are capable of moving. Could it be your *conveniences*??

PEACE be with you, Brothers and Sisters, if you are willing to do what is necessary to get it.

BLACK-SMART

42. "We Have Been Conditioned To Harm Ourselves"

In Part 1 of this essay [Essay 41] we asked each individual about his/her "conveniences", and suggested that these conveniences help keep Black People in last place. We took that approach because many persons feel they are in control of their self-abuse, and can stop that self-abuse whenever they decide to do so (or whenever they are presented with a reason why they should do so). In this essay, we will take a social approach to each individual's self-abuse and, based on what we discover, offer some suggestions that might help some Brothers and Sisters begin to eliminate pot, cigarettes, dope, liquor and unnecessary pills from their diet.

We will begin by stating that you really don't determine that you want to smoke cigarettes or marijuana. You don't come to the conclusion that you want to use birth control pills. No, you don't determine either of these things. This social system (of white people, by white people and for white people) makes these determinations for you, but it does it in such a sneaky way that you don't even realize what is happening.

Our forefathers (Africans) realized that each person is born with a spirit (a will to do what you want to do), and this spirit, combined with an understanding of what goes on around you (a properly developed mind), is the key to each person's inner strength. If your inner strength is allowed to develop, you can resist anything that goes on around you (you can resist efforts to influence you) and do what you want to do, what you have the will to do. However, if your inner strength is not allowed to develop, your tendency will not be to do what you want to do, but to take the easy way out of everything by doing what someone else wants you to do, by settling for other people's solutions to your problems, and by satisfying yourself with what someone else has made available to you. You get into the habit of not really thinking, you do not seek to understand who you are or where your interests lie, and you tend to insist that petty relationships (you to money, you to clothes and cars, etc.) and petty practices (clubbing, getting high, etc.) are the keys to happiness and a complete life. In short, your inner strength is not allowed to develop, the real you is swept under the rug and forgotten and a plastic you, the programmed/controlled you, takes its place. For this reason (because the programmed you is what functions), you do not do what you want to do (the real you is under the rug), you do what those who are in control want you to do.

When We/Black People came into contact with white people, they militarily dominated Us and put forces in motion that would ensure their continued domination of Us. They sought to systematically brainwash Us (mis-develop and under-develop Our minds) and kill Our spirit (Our will to resist them, Our will to be Us). In essence, they sought to take away each Black person's inner strength and succeeded in doing so to a large degree. As they robbed Us of Our inner strength, they simultaneously (at the same time) conditioned Us to harm Ourselves. They then anticipated Our response to their domination and provided Us with some pleasurable but deadly pacifiers. They know how depressed dominated people get, so they made dope and liquor easily accessible to Us. They know dominated persons have problems having fun so they made it easy for Us to get high. They know dominated persons over-sex themselves, and since whites are concerned about "overpopulation", they made pills, diaphragms and sterilization available to Us. They know dominated persons are nervous and unsure of themselves in certain situations, so they made it convenient for Us to calm Ourselves down with cigarettes and sedatives. They also know that dominated people are a threat to their (white people's) secure way-of-life, so they make sure that the pacifiers (liquor, dope, cigarettes, etc.) they give Us will also harm Us. That way they can wipe Us out as they calm Us down, and guarantee security for themselves in the future.

[At this time we will explain that a pacifier is something that is given to a person to keep him from doing something that might cause someone else discomfort. For example, a baby cries because he is hungry, he wants some food. The adult knows the baby is hungry but the adult does not want to fix the food, he does not want to give the baby what the baby wants to have. But in order to get the baby to stop making that noise, the adult puts a pacifier

142   BLACK-SMART

in the baby's mouth. The baby, thinking he has what he wants, stops crying and the adult goes about his comfort undisturbed. A deadly pacifier would not only get the baby to shut up, but also gradually render the baby incapable of making noise. For example, instead of giving the baby a regular pacifier, the adult might stick a sweet tasting pacifier into the baby's mouth that will shut him up now and give him cancer of the throat in the long run. The sweeter the pacifier tastes, the more the baby will suck it; the more the baby sucks, the closer he comes to losing his ability to make noise.]

So, after causing your depression, the social system made a pacifier available to you. You don't decide that you want to make use of the pacifier, you just settle for what the system has offered you.

Look at it this way. If you wanted to control your chances of getting pregnant, would you ask the doctor to make you a birth control pill that would also give you cancer or cause you to bleed inside? We doubt it. If you wanted to get "high", would you ask someone to mix up some leaves that might have anything from roach poison to DDT mixed in with them? We don't think so. If you feel uneasy when you get around certain people, would you ask someone to make you a cigarette that is going to destroy your lungs as it pre-occupies (draws the attention of) you and others? We doubt it. If you are depressed, would you ask someone to make a drink for you that will destroy your brain? We doubt it. But, if you have been made to feel that you are unable to come up with solutions to your depression, and these deadly type things are made available to you, would you accept them? Certainly!

And that is what happened, Brothers and Sisters. Some of you will have trouble accepting this because you don't want to believe that you have been manipulated to that degree, but you have been. We accepted the social system's pacifiers, but in order to maintain Our plastic egos (programmed self-concepts), each of Us insists that he/she decided to do what he/she is doing. This indicates that each of Us is hooked; some critically, some casually, but hooked nonetheless. Each of Us feels an inability to stop doing what We have been programmed to do (no inner strength). One addict feel he has to have a drink or a jay everyday, while another addict might not have anything regularly but feels he has to have something in certain situations (at a party, in a crowd, etc.). Either way the fact remains. You are hooked (while you talk about Black Power) and Black People are coming out with the short end of the stick as a result (if We get any of the stick).

We hope you understand what has been said. This essay is by no means a complete analysis of self-abuse among Black People, but it does approach the problem. Since We, Black People, do not have institutions functioning that will help Us eliminate Our problems, We must take the responsibility of dealing with them individually and collectively (in groups). We should not be ashamed or embarrassed because We have been conditioned to do these things. Instead, each of Us should deal with whoever or whatever he/she feels he/she needs to deal with in order to effect/activate the right solution.

We promised we would make some suggestions (you can come up with as many as we can). These suggestions might help persons who can relate to them who want to "break their habit", but they definitely will not help those who do not want to stop abusing themselves.

(1) Do not believe that you can not stop doing what you are presently doing. Since your inner strength is missing, you might feel an inability to resist pot, pills, etc. That feeling of inability is not real. It is only a part of your conditioning. Our enslavers know that as long as you feel an inability to do something, you don't do it simply because you never get to the point of attempting to do it. That feeling stops you before you even start. Overcome that feeling of inability by attempting to resist anyway. That attempt will be the first step toward eliminating the self-abuse. So, don't let a feeling defeat you. Regardless of how/what you feel, attempt to resist anyway.

(2) Recognize that self-abuse is a weakness, and realize that a weak person is constantly taken advantage of. Admit to yourself that you have already been manipulated ("used") by the social system, and decide that you are not going to put yourself in a position to be used anymore. Understand that you have to be alert at all times in order to survive in this hell house; understand that the very moment you are high or drunk might be the moment when some pigs (or an idiot) kick your door down. Understand that you cannot afford to

be "fucked up" in the head when they come.

[1 and 2 might be made easier if you consider certain personal factors: a) Your family/intimate life. Is it satisfactory? b) Your friends. Will their actions hinder you or help you? c) Places you frequent/check out. Maybe they are not suited to your temperament or inner yearnings? d) Yourself. Do you face up to the real motives for what you do? Do you do things in order to be accepted? etc. e) Other. You can fill these in better than we can.

(3) Seek to regain your inner strength, your will to do things that will be good for you. This will lead you to seek your own solutions. It will lead you to an understanding of who you are, and what you have to do to protect yourself from them. Understand the forces that are operating against you and exercise/develop your mind by trying to think of healthy things you can do to counter those forces. Spend your time doing things that will enhance your self-esteem, and substantiate/support the self esteem by relating what you do to what your ancestors did thousands of years ago. This must include learning your history. Black People have a history that will fill each of Us with so much pride. Find out about it; and compare what you discover with what others have discovered by attending classes, speeches, discussions, (which are often free of charge) etc.

(4) Understand that your major problem is a social problem, and that you cannot take a personal approach to a social problem and eliminate that problem. Understand that you have to deal with the system that manufactures people with problems, and do so. Understand that if you do not deal with this system that caused your problems, your sons, daughters, nephews and nieces are going to be affected by problems that will cause them to abuse themselves a lot more than you have abused yourself. Don't think that you can deal with the system overnight or in a couple of years. Prepare yourself to battle against it for a lifetime if necessary. Prepare yourself for victories, setbacks and discouragements, and by so doing, eliminate the probability that you will begin to develop a feeling of hopelessness and, as a result, relapse into the habits your enemy wants you to practice.

(5) Believe in yourself. Let YOU be your guide. You can do whatever you want to do.

PEACE be with you, Brothers and Sisters, if you are willing to do what is necessary to get it.

BLACK-SMART

43. "Let's Get Back To Ourselves"

In this essay we will briefly mention some things Black People need to grasp, individually and collectively, that will help Us make some strides that will benefit Us. The things we will mention will not be new to Black People. As a matter of fact, they were once a part of Black People, a vital part of those Blacks who are responsible for establishing the greatest civilization man has ever experienced. So, in grasping these things today, We will not be experimenting with a new idea; We will instead be getting back to Ourselves. We will be re-acquainting Ourselves with the Virtues that made Our Forefathers the most respected people in the world, and re-acquainting Ourselves with the Virtues that must be a part of Us if We hope to rid Ourselves of these "hard times" and build institutions that will take Us to Humanity-hood/Nationhood/Humanity-hood.

These are the Virtues We, Black People, need to re-acquaint Ourselves with:

(1) Control of Thought [We must be the makers of Our ideas].

(2) Control of Action [We must determine what We will do and what We will not do].

(3) Steadfastness of Purpose [We must establish an objective/objectives and stick with it/them].

(4) Identity With the Higher Ideals in Life [Our philosophy on life and what We attempt to do must not be limited by the circumstances and conditions under which We live].

(5) Evidence of Having a Mission in Life [We must be about an objective, and what We-- each and every one of Us-- do must be a reflection of what We say We are about].

(6) Freedom From Resentment When Under the Experience of Persecution and Wrong [We must maintain a clear head, one which will enable Us to think with clarity and logic, especially when We are under attack].

(7) Confidence in and Respect for Our Leaders [We must support those who represent Us].

(8) Confidence in One's Ability to Learn [Each of Us must believe in

himself/herself. No one among Us should sell himself/herself short].

(9) Readiness or Preparedness for Action   [We must recognize the importance and necessity of organizing, organization, planning and preparation].

These are the Virtues We need to re-acquaint Ourselves with. We will have to re-absorb other qualities as well as We be about the business of properly developing Ourselves, individually and collectively, and moving as "one unified force" to self-determination and Nationhood.

In essays that will be published in a later collection, we will reprint some of the things we have already stated and make additions that we hope will inspire Our People to start taking Our future seriously. We hope to get each of Us to realize how serious the cancers in Our community are (they threaten Our very existence), to realize the necessity of eliminating them, and to resolve Ourselves to work toward their elimination. We hope the readers of these essays will assist us.

PEACE be with you, Brothers and Sisters, if you are willing to do what is necessary to get it.

CONCLUSION

"Peace be with you, Brothers and Sisters, if you are willing to do what is necessary to get it."

Therein lies the salvation of Black People throughout the world. Therein, what each of Us is willing to do, what each individual is willing to do, resides tomorrow's realities for America's sons and daughters of African slaves. We can have peace for Ourselves and Our offspring, but only if We are willing to do what is necessary to get it.

We are not discussing capability here. We are not questioning whether Black People have the capacity to assert themselves/Ourselves. We are not questioning whether Black People have the capacity to impose "Blackness" onto the world arena. No, there is no discussion of capability here because it is well-understood that We, Black People, are capable of doing whatever We want to do. But, are Black People willing??

To do, or not to do; that is the question.

Peace be with you, Brothers and Sisters, if you are willing to do what is necessary to get it. And if you are not willing to do what is necessary, then STOP COMPLAIN-ING!

Other Publications of "THE PEOPLE" include:

TEN LESSONS: AN INTRODUCTION TO BLACK HISTORY.
LESSONS FROM HISTORY ALL BLACK PERSONS SHOULD BE
*   AWARE OF.*
PROFILES IN BLACK.
CONCERNING RELIGION.
THE REPUBLIC OF NEW AFRIKA: ITS DEVELOPMENT,
*   IDEOLOGY AND OBJECTIVES.*
SPOTLIGHT ON MALE/FEMALE RELATIONS.
THE PEOPLE SPEAKS, VOL. 1
THE PEOPLE SPEAKS, VOL. 2
BLACK-SMART